Fenland Waterways

Including the Middle Level
and the Old and New Bedford Rivers

CHRIS HOWES

Imray Laurie Norie & Wilson

Published by
Imray, Laurie, Norie & Wilson Ltd
Wych House, St Ives,
Cambridgeshire PE27 5BT, England
www.imray.com
2020

British Library Cataloguing in Publication Data
A catalogue record for this book is available from the British Library.

ISBN 978 178679 148 1

CAUTION
Every effort has been taken to ensure the accuracy of this book. It
contains selected information and thus is not definitive and does not
include all known information on the subject in hand; this is
particularly relevant to the plans which should not be used for
navigation. The author and publisher believe that its selection is a
useful aid to prudent navigation but the safety of a vessel depends
ultimately on the judgement of the navigator who should assess all
information, published or unpublished, available to him.

This work has been corrected to September 2020

Printed in the UK by Sudbury Print Group

Contents

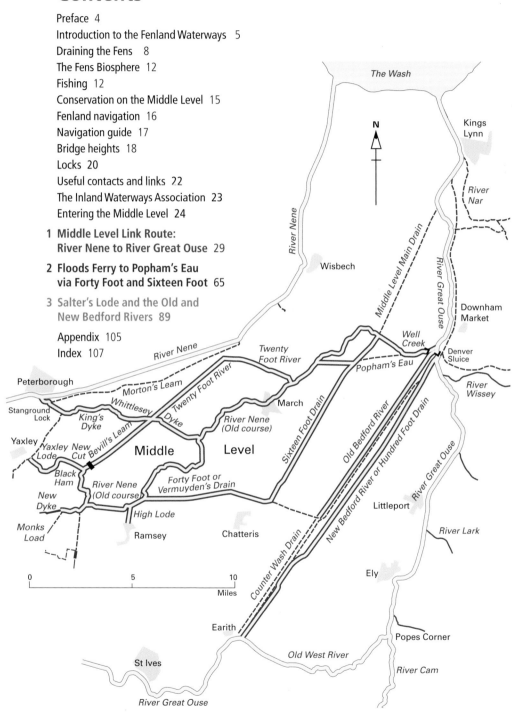

Preface

This book details over 150 miles of navigable fenland waterways, including all the navigable waters of the Middle Level, and the Old and New Bedford Rivers. These beautiful waters, situated in the seemingly remote east of England offer great cruising, huge skies and fantastic sunsets.

This completely rewritten guide provides a practical guide to entering and leaving the Level, licensing, where to moor, shop, and to find services. It also introduces the reader to the unique and fascinating history of the area.

I would like to thank the Middle Level Commissioners, Peter Beckenham, Paul at Salter's Lode, Tina at Stanground, Fox Narrowboats, the Middle Level Watermens' Club, The Well Creek Trust, Andrew Hunter Blair, Peter Cox, John Revell, Mike Daines, and members of Peterborough Branch IWA. I'd also like to express my gratitude to the team at Imray for giving me the opportunity to write this guide, and for converting my enthusiastic ramblings into understandable content.

The author sculling on the Sixteen Foot

The author

Chris Howes has spent most of his life on, and often unintentionally in, the water, messing about in boats. A few years ago he graduated from small self propelled boats up to a larger motorised boat, when he and his wife bought a narrowboat built on the Middle Level. The boat and he are these days rarely parted!

Chris is a former Chairman of Peterborough Branch IWA and regularly writes about, and photographs, waterways, and waterway issues.

Introduction to the Fenland Waterways

What are The Fens, and where are they?

This book details the waterways between the Rivers Nene and Great Ouse, describes the surrounding countryside and endeavours to introduce some of the rich and varied history of the area.

At the largest scale, the Fens are an area of low-lying land in eastern England, once inundated with water, but now largely drained. They comprise over 1,200 square miles, bounded in the west by the limestone hills of the Midlands, to the south and east by the chalk hills of Cambridgeshire, Norfolk and Suffolk, and in the north the Fens meet the North Sea at the Wash.

Welney Washes

The Bedford Levels

The term 'The Bedford Levels' described an area, sometimes known as 'The Great Fen', of 703 sq. miles which fell within the general description of 'The Fens'. It was drained in the 17th century by a group of investors led by Francis Russell, the 4th Duke of Bedford.

The term the North Level described the area between the River Welland and the River Nene.

The Middle Level is the area between the River Nene (in the north) and the Old Bedford River (in the south).

The South Level was the land between the Old Bedford River and River Great Ouse.

The Middle Level, one of the three subdivisions of the Bedford Levels, is now the fourth largest navigation authority in the United Kingdom. The North Level remains as an Internal Drainage Board, and the South Level having ceased to exist (other than as an occasional descriptive term) when the Bedford Level Corporation was wound up in the 1920s.

The term 'Fenland Waterways' generally describes the areas drained by Cornelius Vermuyden in the 17th century, and now largely administered by, and falling under the responsibility of, the Middle Level Commissioners.

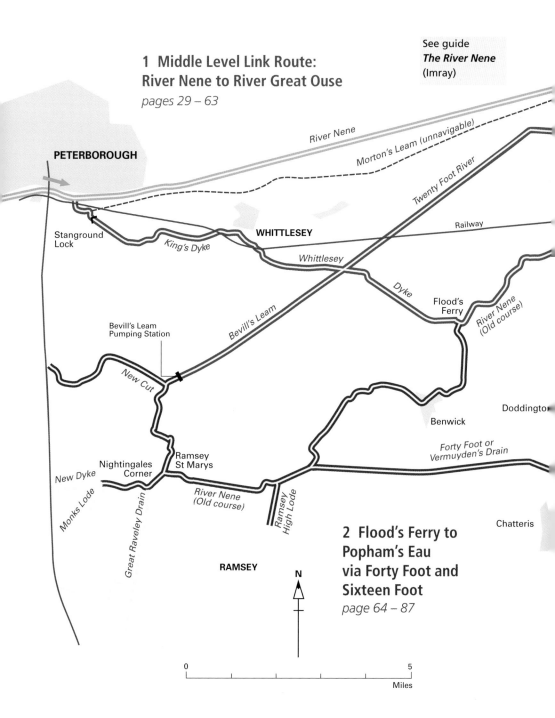

1 Middle Level Link Route: River Nene to River Great Ouse

pages 29 – 63

See guide
The River Nene
(Imray)

River Nene

Morton's Leam (unnavigable)

PETERBOROUGH

Twenty Foot River

Stanground Lock

Railway

King's Dyke

WHITTLESEY

Whittlesey

Dyke

Flood's Ferry

River Nene (Old course)

Bevill's Leam Pumping Station

Bevill's Leam

New Cut

Doddington

Benwick

Ramsey St Marys

Forty Foot or Vermuyden's Drain

Nightingales Corner

New Dyke

River Nene (Old course)

Ramsey High Lode

Monks Lode

Great Raveley Drain

Chatteris

RAMSEY

N

2 Flood's Ferry to Popham's Eau via Forty Foot and Sixteen Foot

page 64 – 87

0   5

Miles

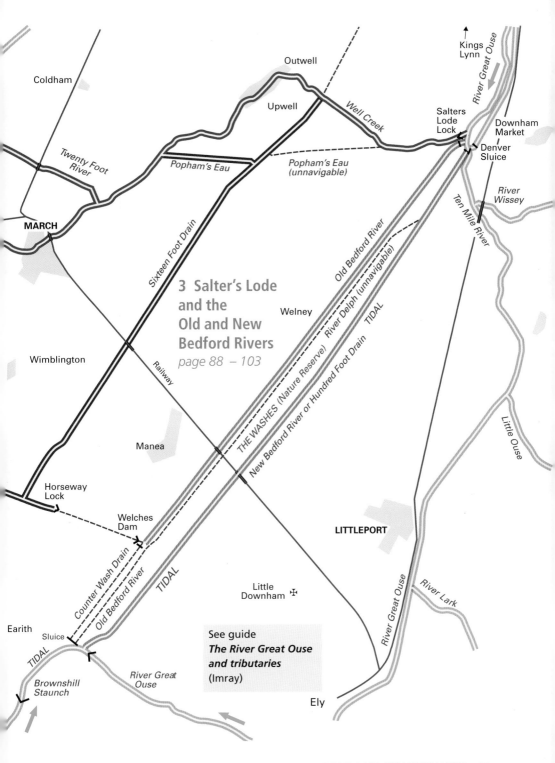

Coldham

Outwell

Upwell

Well Creek

Kings Lynn

River Great Ouse

Salters Lode Lock

Downham Market

Denver Sluice

Twenty Foot River

Popham's Eau

Popham's Eau (unnavigable)

River Wissey

MARCH

Sixteen Foot Drain

Ten Mile River

Old Bedford River

River Delph (unnavigable)

3 Salter's Lode and the Old and New Bedford Rivers
page 88 – 103

Welney

THE WASHES (Nature Reserve)

TIDAL

Wimblington

Railway

New Bedford River or Hundred Foot Drain

Little Ouse

Manea

LITTLEPORT

Horseway Lock

Welches Dam

Counter Wash Drain

Old Bedford River

TIDAL

Little Downham

River Great Ouse

River Lark

Earith

Sluice

TIDAL

See guide
The River Great Ouse and tributaries
(Imray)

Brownshill Staunch

River Great Ouse

Ely

Draining the Fens

The landscape of the Fens has been shaped by man's actions. It is no more natural than, for example, central London. So how have we come to turn a marshy wetland wrapped in fog and mist, into what we have today? Where should one begin the story of the Fens?

We will start at the end of the last Ice Age, 10,000 years ago. The melting of the ice raised sea levels, and some time around 6,500BC Britain's land bridge with Europe, Doggerland, disappeared under the sea, and a coastline took shape along what we now call East Anglia.

By 5,000BC the Fens had become covered by a huge forest that was to stand for thousands of years, and by 2,000BC, the Fens were drying out and population was gradually increasing. The Bronze Age encampment at Flag Fen, near Peterborough, dates from around 1500BC and proves not only that by this period man was living on the Fen edge, but that he was starting to control his wetland environment.

In 43AD the Romans arrived in the Fens and started to manage the landscape, digging ditches and dykes (including Car Dyke) and building embankments and sea defences (the eponymously named Roman Bank). After the Roman withdrawal from Britain in 410AD, the Fens reverted to a wilderness of meres and marshes. Drainage and wetland management never really engaged the Anglo-Saxon invaders' interest.

By 600BC another wet period was affecting all of Europe, and the Fens became a lot wetter and even more difficult to inhabit. These periodical wet periods caused the trees and vegetation to die and fall. This was the source of the peat. Many of the trunks were preserved in airless waterlogged conditions and ploughed out as 'bog oaks' right up to the mid twentieth century.

The inundation of water was such that when in 669AD Guthlac, the 26 year-old son of a Mercian nobleman, resolved to become a hermit and prove his faith and devotion by living on a remote island. He was sainted and two years later, suffering from ague and marsh fever, Guthlac died. In 716AD construction of Crowland Abbey began on the island.

In 731AD the Venerable Bede described Ely as 'surrounded on all sides by sea and Fens' and resembling 'an island surrounded by water and marshes'. The monk Felix wrote of 'a most dismal Fen of immense size … consisting of marshes, now of bogs, sometimes of black waters overhung by fog, sometimes studded with wooded islands and traversed by the windings of tortuous streams'.

In 793AD Viking raids on the east of England began. By 869AD they had occupied all of East Anglia, which became part of the Danelaw, ceded by King Alfred to the Danes in 878AD, but reconquered by Alfred's grandson Eadred in 955AD. The Vikings, in addition to being famed sailors, displayed practical skills in water management. Around 1020 King Canute instructed the cutting of King's Dyke near Whittlesey. Apparently the King had experienced a rough crossing of the great Whittlesey Mere and required a smoother and more comfortable passage (a not very 'tough guy Viking' attitude!).

Between the 13th and 15th centuries the Fens became very wet again. The Wash coast had been gradually retreating back from Wisbech and Ely as a result of both fluvial and marine siltation. At the same time many trees were being felled in the Midlands, causing run-off into the rivers to increase, whilst Midland rivers were straightened to facilitate waterborne trade. In consequence yet more water was arriving in the Fens. These rivers were generally fast flowing as they ran down from the hills, but then slowed down in the flat Fens, depositing silt and blocking the river's course to the sea. The more water that arrived, the more it backed up.

In 1216 King John lost his treasure in the marshes near Wisbech (see p. 61).

John's successor Henry III appointed the first 'Commissions of Sewers' in 1258 in order to lead a unified approach to drainage. Despite this, in 1236 and 1260 exceptionally high tides drowned hundreds of people. A dead whale was washed up on the shores of Wisbech.

In 1400, shortly after Henry IV's accession to the throne, Wisbech was very nearly washed away by floods, and the Commissions of Sewers were granted new rights to collect taxes to raise funds for drainage schemes, and given powers to punish tax evaders. These powers were extended in 1427, but by the 1500s the Fens were subject to regular years of flooding.

Most local drainage schemes were initiated and managed by the great monasteries that populated the Fens. In 1487 John Morton, Bishop of Ely, had Morton's Leam cut, which straightened the River Nene north east of Peterborough. This was intended to reduce the silting at the port of Wisbech which was then still on the coast. Morton had plans for further drainage works, but these were halted by the Wars of the Roses.

Henry VIII's dissolution of the monasteries, between 1536 and 1541, created an administrative vacuum and the former co-ordinated approach to clearing out ditches disappeared (some land owners did, but often their neighbours didn't bother) and matters once again deteriorated, and the Fens became wetter once more. In 1570, during exceptionally high tides, the sea breached Roman Bank between Wisbech and Walsoken, and flooding penetrated over 50 miles inland, as far as Bedford!

From 1600 to 1630 the area was subject to almost continual flooding. In 1600 a General Drainage Act was passed, and in 1605 Popham's Eau was dug in an attempt to drain the area around Upwell. However there was little further activity until in 1630 a group of investors, lead by Francis Russell, 4th Earl of Bedford, formed as 'Gentlemen Adventurers'. They looked to Holland for expertise in drainage and employed the Dutchman, Cornelius Vermuyden, to drain the Fens.

Vermuyden embarked on a course of straightening rivers, to increase their flow, as well as having new rivers cut including 'Vermuyden's Drain' (now more commonly called the Forty Foot) and the Bedford River. They were designed to move water on more quickly towards the sea.

The original idea was that the drainage would only be sufficient to keep the land dry during the summer months. Some of the Adventurers welcomed the prospect of continued water inundation every winter, anticipating the same benefits to the land that result from the annual Nile floods in Egypt. Sadly they didn't appreciate that while the Nile's fresh waters deposit nutrient rich material which fertilised the land, winter flooding in the Fens mixed sea and river water and this brackish water didn't have anything like the same nutritional benefits. In 1637 Fen drainage was declared 'complete'. The area was optimistically christened with the descriptive name 'the summer lands'. But the measures were only partly effective in keeping the land dry during summer and there were several bad floods during the English Civil War.

After the Civil War a new Drainage Act required William, 5th Earl (and now also 1st Duke) of Bedford to make the land capable of supporting farming throughout the entire year. Vermuyden was again put in charge, and he divided the area into three administrative regions, the North Level (between the River Glen and Morton's Leam, just south of the current course of the River Nene), The Middle Level (south of the North Level down to the Old Bedford River), and the South Level (to the south and east of the Bedford River).

Major new engineering works were undertaken including constructing the Sixteen Foot Drain, the Twenty Foot River, the Forty Foot Drain, and the New Bedford River (aka the Hundred Foot River). Digging the New Bedford River created a 5,600 acre reservoir bordered on the west by the (Old) Bedford River. The works were completed in 1652. Water from further inland, Bedford, St Neots, St Ives and Huntingdon no longer spilled into the Fens, contributing to their flooding, but was carried straight out into the estuary of the Great Ouse below Denver.

Fairly soon after the second draining of the Fens, a phenomenon occurred which for several years puzzled everybody. It appeared that the rivers were rising up out of the surrounding land. Eventually it was realised that the rivers weren't actually going up, but that the land, which was mainly peat, was sinking as it dried out. Much of the land of the Middle Level is believed to have dropped a total of 7 metres (20 feet) since before Vermuyden started work in the mid Seventeenth Century (some of which is evidenced by the Holme Post, installed in 1851 (see p. 74).

The Fens became an 'upside down world' where the rivers were higher than the land they were intended to drain. This imposed two unanticipated requirements: raised river banks have had to be regularly strengthened ever since and water had to be raised by 'engines' from the fields into the drains above them. Initially this pumping was by horse driven scoop wheels, or by 'windmills'. By 1758 there were 250 of these windscoops in the mid-Fens. It was said that wherever one went in the Fens, one could see twenty or thirty 'windmills'.

Prior to Vermuyden most of the water in the Fens eventually ran out into the sea in a great Estuary north of Wisbech which the Roman geographer Ptolemy had called Metaire. The digging of the Old and New Bedford rivers and diversion of the Ouse to join the sea at King's Lynn changed this.

In 1713 the collapse of the Denver Sluice built by Vermuyden forced the water from the Bedford River back up the Ely Ouse. The Sluice was not rebuilt until 1750.

In 1723 the author of Robinson Crusoe, Daniel Defoe, observed 'All the waters of the middle part of England that do not run into the Thames or Trent come down into these Fens' describing the area as 'the sink of no less than 13 counties'.

The foggy, damp atmosphere of the Fens had an adverse effect on health. The 'marsh miasma' or ' Fen-ague' was believed to be carried in the bad air. The illness is now believed to have been malaria, spread by mosquitoes that thrived in the stagnant marsh water. Defoe observed, 'for 'tis a horrid air for a stranger to breathe in'. Those that survived the infection often suffered again from its symptoms. Samuel Pepys was a famous sufferer as was Oliver Cromwell who died from Tertian Ague, aged 59.

In 1820 steam driven pumps were installed in the Fens. Not being wind reliant, they continued pumping irrespective of whether the wind was blowing, and gradually replaced the windscoops. Steam pumps facilitated the mid 19th-century draining of the meres or lakes which had survived earlier drainage (see **The Lost Meres** on page 74). In 1851 Whittlesey Mere was drained.

In 1851 the Commissions of Sewers was brought to an end, and management was transferred to the newly formed Middle Level Commissioners.

Steam power was replaced by diesel in the 1930–40s. The last working boat on the Middle Level *Shellfen* was a Dutch built barge which had originally carried bulbs in the Netherlands, but was brought to the Fens and converted to carry fuel to the many small pumping stations draining the Level (see p. 81).

In the 1950s electric pumps became more widespread as a quieter and cleaner alternative to diesel and in 1974 *Shellfen* was retired from fuel delivery, sold and moved to the Bridgewater canal. She was restored in 2019 in Gloucester.

The Fenland landscape is filled again with the appearance of 'windmills', now in the form of wind turbines, and producing far more electricity than needed for drainage pumps.

As Vermuyden designed it, the Middle Level was all on one level (no locks) and drained entirely by gravity. Most of the water ran off at two points, at Welches Dam - into the Old Bedford River, and at Salter's Lode from the Well Creek. It arrived at Welches Dam via the Forty Foot river and the Horseway Channel, and it arrived at Well Creek along Popham's Eau which joined the Well Creek at Nordelph. The Old Bedford River itself discharges into the Ouse just above Salter's Lode, so the water all arrived at the same destination, albeit by different routes. As the Middle Level dried out and the land sank, gravity discharge decreased in efficiency.

The 1844 Middle Level Act allowed for the lowering of the centre section of the Level, which is why we now have locks at Whittlesey (Ashline), Marmont Priory and Welches Dam. A new drain was cut, extending the Sixteen Foot north from its junction with Popham's Eau at Three Holes up to Wiggenhall St Germans. The Sixteen Foot and Forty Foot Rivers were also linked. A new 'Middle Level Main Drain' was cut, running north to Wiggenhall St Germans, near Kings Lynn, where tide levels could be up to 7 feet lower than at Salter's Lode. Well Creek is carried across the Main Drain on Mullicourt Aqueduct.

The Middle Level Main Drain, which emptied into the River Ouse through sluices at Eau Brink Water, was discharged only at low tide. In 1862 the sluice collapsed, allowing the sea to reclaim large areas of marshland. In 1951 a pumping station was constructed next to the repaired sluices with three powerful diesel pumps. Two further electric pumps were added in 1951, which finally marked the end of gravity discharge.

In the 1980s a pumping station was built across Bevill's Leam at Pondersbridge, and by 2005 it was felt that increased run-off, continued land shrinkage, and an upturn in development required a greater pumping capacity. A new pumping station was built at St. Germans downstream from the original with a discharge capacity of 100 tonnes of water per second and is the largest pumping station in the country. The Middle Level today is drained by over 100 pumping stations. Every drop of water is pumped a minimum of twice, once from a field side drain into a main drain, and a second time out of the Main Drain at St Germans into the Great Ouse. Water from the west of the Level is three-times pumped, having also been lifted at Bevill's Leam. The battles to remove water from low lying land, and to prevent the sea coming in and reclaiming its former territories continue.

Between 1930 and 1954 £10 million was spent raising and strengthening banks. Major floods occurred in 1936, 1937 and 1939, whilst 1947 witnessed the biggest flood for over a century with 10 square miles disappearing under water. In 1953 another disastrous flood took 307 lives in the East of England.

Vermuyden had further proposed an extra channel, running east of the Great Ouse and joining it below Denver, but this wasn't built in his time. The great engineer, John Rennie, made a similar suggestion in 1810, and in 1963 the Relief Channels and Cut Off Channels were opened, which in winter redirects the headwaters of the Rivers Lark, Little Ouse and Wissey. This completed Vermuyden's vision, on almost exactly the line he had drawn it nearly 300 years earlier.

Some argue that this demonstrates Vermuyden's visionary genius, others, that it was simply obvious. The geologist Sydney Skertchly remarked in 1877 'Vermuyden began badly, progressed ignorantly, and finished disastrously'. I sometimes think 'if you dig enough ditches, eventually you must end up with something that works'. Whether you consider Vermuyden was brilliant or flawed, we can't deny that he permanently changed the landscape of Fenland. It would be wrong to consider the draining of the Fens a static task, which has essentially been completed. It requires continual work, reinforcing and raising river banks and dredging out silted up channels. This 'never ending task' is shared by the Environment Agency, Middle Level Commissioners, and a plethora of IDBs (Internal Drainage Boards).

What's in a name?

Fenland has had many nicknames over the years and each one sheds a different light on the various aspects of its history.

In Medieval times the area had a number of major ecclesiastical establishments, including Crowland, Ramsey, Chatteris and Thorney Abbeys, as well as Ely and Peterborough Cathedrals. Reflecting this ample provision for the spiritual, the name **The Holy Land of the English** was applied.

Prior to Vermuyden's draining of the Fens, the area was often referred to as **The Great Eastern Swamp**, or **The Old Drowned Lands**.

Vermuyden's first drainage scheme was intended to provide relief from flooding during summer months and gave rise to the description **The Summer Lands**.

During WWII the productive rich black soil of the Fens was put to use feeding the country, which was in danger of going hungry as the German blockade of shipping tightened. The area then acquired the deserved nickname **The Breadbasket of Britain**.

The flat countryside, devoid of hills to disturb its great panoramic landscapes, has given rise to the name **The Land of the Three-quarter Sky**.

And because none of the other publishers of Waterways Guides cover the Fens, we like to think of it as **Imray Country!**

The Fens Biosphere

A Biosphere is an internationally recognised designation awarded by UNESCO to a region which has a strong cultural and landscape identity. There are already seven Biospheres in the UK, but none in the east of England.

The aim is for Fenland to attain Biosphere status by 2022, joining a global network of 701 Biospheres in 124 countries.

The goal is to achieve 'a sustainable living fens landscape, supporting more and better spaces for nature and better places for people to live, work and enjoy'. The first task has been to define the area the designation should apply to. This has been done, and the project has achieved the first stage – being granted candidate status.

www.fensbiosphere.org.uk

Fishing

Fishing is a popular activity in Fenland Waters and the Middle Level boasts a full range of fresh water fish, including roach, bream, tench, pike and eels.

Overall authority resides with the Environment Agency, from whom rod licences must be obtained. Some waters are rented to different angling clubs who have exclusive use. These offer either full membership, or day membership to visitors. Other waters, for example, Well Creek, are open to anyone with a rod licence. The Middle Level Commissioners publish a list and map. Details of the various clubs are readily available on line.

The closed season between 15 March & 15 June that restricts fishing nationally on all Environment Agency waters also applies to the Middle Level.

Local angling clubs regularly organise competitions, and the British Pike Championships (the largest predator competiton in Europe) are held every year near Whittlesey.

Conservation on the Middle Level

What's so special about a fen drain?

There is a lot more to the fenland environment than initially meets the eye. The open, windswept plain, scoured, squashed, swamped and then saved over millennia, is now a fertile patchwork of farms, fields and villages, deftly shaped by the actions of man. In such conditions, wildlife needs to find niches in which to thrive – places where shelter, food and mobility can be found. In the fens this often means looking down, into the labyrinthine maze of ditches, drains and rivers.

The Middle Level area covers roughly 270 square miles and includes 120 miles of main river and over 550 miles of adjacent channels and ditches managed by the Commissioners and Internal Drainage Boards. Within the different depths, profiles, lengths and habitat features there are conditions sought by a host of fascinating species, some common and some increasingly rare.

From early spring, water voles begin emerging more regularly from their burrows just above the water's edge to browse new shoots of reed and grass. The Middle Level is home to an important population of this protected species which nationally has undergone a steep decline in the last century. Although rarely seen (hearing a loud 'plop' as they dive under water is as close as you may get) their feeding signs and latrines are easily recognisable for anyone scanning riparian margins. The Middle Level Commissioners take care in our work to leave the water vole's habitat as undisturbed as possible and employ a sensitive mowing and cleansing regime to ensure this. It isn't an easy life for a water vole as predatory American mink are still found in our waterways. We monitor closely for signs of this non-native invasive species. Of similar appearance and just as secretive is the beautiful otter which has returned from the brink of extinction to once again find a home in our waterways.

Our banks are vital corridors of habitat and the region is home to a good densities of bird species such as kingfisher, great crested grebe and barn owl. The grassy strips of bankside vegetation, many of which are cut on rotation, offer superb hunting grounds for the latter in particular. But if there is one species from our waterways that perhaps stirs the imagination most, silkily threading its way through layers of fenland history and folklore, it is the European eel. Elusive in nature and wonderfully mysterious in its epic life cycle, we monitor the population in our drains and research ways to make our pumps 'eel friendly'.

Next time you pass through, drop your eyes from the horizon momentarily and consider the ponderous waters of the Middle Level. Ask yourself 'what's so special about a fen drain'?

The Conservation Officer is always keen to receive sightings or photographs of wildlife in the Middle Level:
peter.beckenham@middlelevel.gov.uk

Peter Beckenham,
Conservation Officer for Middle Level
Commissioners, February 2020

Fenland navigation

The quiet waters and stunning landscapes of the Middle Level feel more remote than most of the rest of the country's network of navigable inland waterways. To many this is their beauty and their attraction. However it is important to remember this very remoteness when planning your trip. The Middle Level will have everything you may reasonably need - moorings, shops, water points, diesel, pump out and elsan disposal, rubbish disposal, but fewer, and further apart, than you may be used to. Don't rely on just being able to 'pop out for milk'; ensure you have sufficient stocks and plan your journey.

Taking the slow route

The two entry (or exit) points of the Middle Level (Stanground, and Salter's Lode Sluice), are joined by the 'Link Route' which forms the quickest route to transit between the Rivers Nene and Great Ouse. This is a journey of approximately nine hours. However the rich and diverse landscape of the Fens rewards a longer visit, so why not take the slow route and explore more of the 120 miles of waters that constitute the Level?

Weed warning – the waters of the Middle Level do not experience significant flow during the summer months, and rather like canals, are prone to weed growth in warm weather.

The concentration of boat movement, and weed clearance by the Commissioners, tends to keep the Link Route open, but bear in mind that there is a seasonal risk of weed on other waters.

Forty Foot River near Chatteris

Navigation guide

Boat licensing and registration (paying to use the waters)

For many years there was no charge for boating on the Middle Level. This provided no incentive to the Middle Level Commissioners to invest in the provision of boaters' facilities (the Commissioners interests being largely agricultural – draining water in winter and providing irrigation in summer).

In November 2016 the Commissioners submitted a Private Bill to Parliament to enable them to better monitor and regulate navigation. The Bill was revived, following the June 2017 General Election, and finally received Royal Assent and became an Act of Parliament on 1st November 2018.

From 2020 boaters on the Middle Level, whether visitors or resident, need to obtain a licence from the Commissioners which can be obtained by submitting an application form downloaded from the website below and by paying the applicable fee. The intention of the Commissioners, going forward, is to enter into a reciprocal arrangement with the Environment Agency where holders of a valid enhanced EA licence (or CRT Gold Licence) will not need to pay extra to transit the Middle Level. Please check the MLC website for the latest information on this. The benefits of the Middle Level Act to boaters will be several. Some of the income from licencing will be reinvested in the provision of more boating facilities. All boats will have to be insured and hold current boat safety certificates – leading to greater safety for all!

www.middlelevel.gov.uk

Middle Level Commissioner's Navigation Notes – A MUST!

The Commissioners annually publish Navigation Notes, which are available free on their website above.

At the time of publication you could also ask for a free paper copy when you enter the level at either Stanground or Salter's Lode. These notes include useful information on the waters.

Middle Level Commissioners,
Middle Level Offices,
85 Whittlesey Road,
March, Cambs, PE15 0AH
01354 653232
Email enquiries@middlelevel.gov.uk

Fenland District Council

Fenland District Council (FDC) is a middle tier local government authority which administers 210 sq. miles, which includes the market towns of March, Chatteris, Whittlesey and Wisbech. Wisbech sometimes styles itself 'The Capital of the Fens'.

Its administrative area falls largely within the Middle Level.

www.fenland.gov.uk

Bridge heights

Caution

Published bridge headrooms are averages, not minimums. Actual headroom may be significantly less than the published height.

The **Middle Level Commissioners' Navigation Notes** include a table of average bridge headrooms. There are several low bridges on the Middle Level, and great care should be taken when approaching them.

The Middle Level largely consists of man-made drainage channels. The water levels function more like rivers than canals – rising after rain, and gradually falling as they perform their drainage function.

Headrooms can significantly vary on a day to day basis, and sometimes even from hour to hour. Bridges don't include height boards hence the need for care – even if your vessel has previously passed underneath it. Levels at any one bridge can vary by up to 6 inches (150mm). Even the wind can effect water levels.

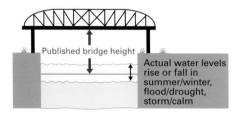

On one occasion the local Peterborough Branch IWA undertook an Easter cruise, mooring one night at Benwick. There was a brisk wind through the night, and in the morning several boats which had happily floated onto moorings the evening before, found themselves grounded! A strong westerly wind can literally 'blow the water down to the other end of the Level'!

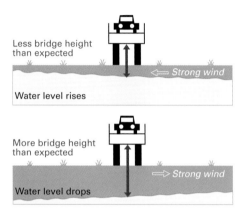

Strong winds from certain directions can 'push' the water into or out of the waterways, making the water levels rise or fall.

There are different summer and winter levels, the former being higher. Winter levels are kept lower to increase capacity for extra flood water storage when needed. The guide to bridge heights is based on the summer levels. It is a navigator's responsibility to assess whether their vessel can safely pass under each bridge, and the advice is always to **slow down** and display **caution**.

Bridges requiring extra vigilance

Caution should be applied to every bridge, but specific 'baddies' are:

On the Link Route:
Bridges in **Well Creek** at **Upwell** and **Outwell**

On the Sixteen Foot:
Boots Bridge and **Bedlam Bridge**

On the Old River Nene:
White Fen Bridge (South of the junction with Whittlesey Dyke)

On the Twenty Foot:
There are **three low bridges**, one of which, **Infield's Bridge**, is only 5'2" (1·6m) and even the most intrepid navigator should think carefully before using this navigation

West of Lodes End Lock:
There are several low bridges demanding caution

Maximum craft dimensions

Height above water
See both 'Bridge heights' and 'Bridges requiring extra vigilance'.
Display caution with all boats, and extra caution if their air draft exceeds 6ft.

Depth below water
Maximum draught varies with water height any one day and how recently the reach was dredged.
Some sections of Well Creek in Upwell and Outwell are narrow and relatively shallow.
One historic boat, drawing 3'6", attending the St Neots IWA Festival of Water in 2018, crossed through the Middle Level but experienced difficulty in Well Creek.

Width
The narrowest locks on the Link Route were built to 11'6" (3·5m). Lodes End Lock is 10'8" (3·3m).

Length
On the main Link Route 70' (21·3m) boats can be accommodated comfortably.

Size
No craft should be longer than 21·3m (70'), or wider than 3·0m (9'10")

Salter's Lode Lock is only 62' (18·9m) long but longer boats can pass through on the level (with the gates at both ends open, when the tide on the Great Ouse is at the same height as Well Creek). Lodes End Lock is 67' (20·7m).

Winding points

These are few and far between, but the helmsman of the longer boat is well advised to take advantage of any opportunity offered by the navigation widening or the junction of two waterways.

Mooring

Unlike our canals, simply stopping and mooring wherever you can get to the bank is not an option on the Middle Level. This shouldn't pose a problem, but like most aspects of the Middle Level requires that little bit more planning in advance. Free short stay public moorings, are provided by the Fenland District Council, Parish Councils, and the Well Creek Trust.

Locks

Entering locks

None of the locks on the Middle Level are wide enough to accept two narrowboats side by side. By extension, none of the lock gates are large enough to allow a narrowboat to enter a lock with only one gate open. Remember: **always open both gates!**

Great Ouse/Well Creek
Salter's Lode
Attended ☎ 01366 382292
Length 18·9m (62')
Width 3·8m (12'5")
Passage for craft up to 24·3m (80') on level water and when tidal conditions allow.

River Nene Old Course
Marmont Priory
Unattended
Length 28·0m (91'10")
Width 3·65 (11')
Care must be taken to keep clear of upstream sill and the downstream access walkway.

Lodes End
Unattended
Length 20.7m (67' 11")
Width 3.3m (10'10")
This is in effect a 'stop lock' with only a small rise.

Whittlesey Dyke
Ashline
Unattended
Length 27·4m (89'11")
Width 3·5m (11'6")

Hold boats at least 1m (3'3") clear of upstream doors to avoid sill and away from downstream doors to avoid entrapment under walkway.

King's Dyke/River Nene
Stanground
Attended - call 24h in advance
☎ 07824 600470
Length 24·4m (80')
Width 3·5m (11'6")

Forty Foot/Vermuyden's Drain
Horseway
Unattended
Length 18·3m (60')
Width 3·65m (12')
(currently closed)

Welches Dam
Unattended
Length 14·3m (47')
Width 3·35m (11')
(currently closed)

Note
A sharp bend at Whittlesey restricts narrow boat length to 21·3m (70').

It is emphasised that lock dimensions should be treated as a guide. If the vessel's dimensions approach those listed on page 19, navigators must proceed with extreme caution.

The Boater's Handbook

In association with the Environment Agency and British Marine, the Canal & River Trust has launched a new edition of The Boater's Handbook. It is an incredibly useful resource for any boater, from novices to old hands alike. The Handbook is written for boat owners and hirers and contains lots of 'getting started' tips as well as important information about how to boat safely. It is intended to refresh memories and to be kept on board your boat as a handy reference guide.

The Trust wants all boaters to be aware of the key safety messages:

- **Avoid slips and trips!** Watch out for ropes, bollards, holes and other hazards, use grab rails and wear non-slip shoes. Don't try to jump from the boat onto the bank and wear a lifejacket if you can't swim.

- **Don't get crushed!** Keep your body out the way of a moving boat: don't fend off with your arms, legs or boat pole, and don't have limbs dangling over the side or your head out the hatch. Keep off the roof when you're underway.

- **Watch out for fire and fumes!** If you smell exhaust, gas, or petrol fumes raise the alert right away. Switch off appliances when you're not using them and keep ventilators open and free of obstructions. Remember that carbon monoxide poisoning is extremely dangerous: early signs include headaches, tiredness, sickness and dizziness, and anyone affected should get medical help right away.

- **Don't rock the boat!** Think carefully before climbing onto the cabin roof as the boat could become top heavy and roll over, and don't all stand together on the same side if it risks tipping the boat over.

- **Remember your lifejacket!** The water is often colder and deeper than you think.

A downloadable copy of the Handbook, and a video setting out key information, can be found on the Canal & River Trust web site, or a copy ordered by contacting CRT customer services

☎ 0303 040 4040
customer.services@canalrivertrust.org.uk

Speed limits

Maximum speed 5mph (8km/h) except between Salter's Lode Lock and Marmont Priory Lock and between Stanground Lock and Turningtree Bridge (after Whittlesey) where the maximum speed is 4mph (6·4km/h).

Covid-19

At the time of going to print, the impact of Covid-19 continues to unfold. In particular, pubs may be closed, so do phone ahead to check.

Useful contacts and links

Inland Waterways Association
☎ 01494 783453

River & Canal Rescue
☎ 01785 785680

Navigation Authorities

Middle Level Commissioners
☎ 01354 653232
Navigation Officer – Kevin Russell
☎ 07725 134170
kevin.russell@middlelevel.gov.uk

Environment Agency Anglian Area
☎ 0370 850 6506

Environment Agency Emergency Number
☎ 0800 706050

Environment Agency SSA Hotline
☎ 0345 988 1188

Locks

Salter's Lode Lock
☎ 01366 382292

Stanground Lock
☎ 078424 600470 / 01733 566413

Denver Lock
☎ 01366 382340

Middle Level overnight moorings

Benwick Old River Nene

March   Old River Nene
             Town Quay
             Marylebone Bridge

Nordelph Gladys Dack's, Well Creek

Ramsey High Lode, off Old River Nene

Salter's Lode Well Creek

Three Holes Sixteen Foot drain

Outwell Basin Well Creek

Upwell outside St Peter's Church, Well Creek

Whittlesey King's Dyke – rear of Leisure Centre

Middle Level marinas

Floods Ferry Marina
Long term mooring only
☎ 01354 677303
www.floodsferrymarina.co.uk

Fox Narrowboats
Moorings, diesel, gas, pump out, workshop, chandlery
☎ 01354 652770
www.foxboats.co.uk

Bill Fen Marina, Ramsey
Moorings, diesel, gas, pump out, chandlery (June 2020)
☎ 01487 813621
www.billfenmarina.com

Middle Level water, pump out and Elsan disposal

Public pump out **March Sanitary Station** requires same token as EA pump-outs, available from:
Fenland District Council One Stop Shop 8 Broad St, March PE15 8TP.
Marina pump outs at **Fox Narrowboats** and **Bill Fen Marina**. Water at **Upwell**.

The Inland Waterways Association

INLAND WATERWAYS ASSOCIATION

The Inland Waterways Association (IWA) was born from necessity back in 1945, when two forward-thinking canal enthusiasts, Tom Rolt and Robert Aickman, realised there was a need to protect the waterways of Britain, which were being abandoned and filled in at an alarming rate in favour of new road and railway networks. At a meeting in August 1945, at Tardebigge, near Bromsgrove on the Worcester and Birmingham Canal, plans for IWA were agreed between the two men and the Association was officially set up in February 1946. In November of that year, the first ever Bulletin was issued informing members that the Stratford Canal, Kennet and Avon and Suffolk Stour were the targets of the first IWA campaigns.

On the Stratford Canal, Rolt successfully challenged Great Western Railway (GWR), the then owners of the Stratford Canal, at Tunnel Lane, Lifford Bridge at Kings Norton. GWR had replaced a former drawbridge with a new bridge that was too low to allow boat passage along the canal, despite a statutory right of navigation existing. A question in Parliament and a notice of intention to navigate, forced GWR to lift the bridge to allow Rolt, in his narrowboat Cressy to pass.

The successes of these early actions gave IWA the confidence needed to start campaigning far and wide, further buoyed by the rise of leisure boating, which swelled membership numbers during the 1950s, 60s and beyond.

Today, IWA speaks for all users of the inland waterways network, which includes 6,500 miles of rivers and canals across England and Wales as well as the Scottish Canals. IWA works tirelessly to help protect and restore these waterways through its lobbying and campaigning activity, whether on a government level, with changes to legislation or the introduction of new transport initiatives, or on a more local level with council-led planning issues or decisions from navigation authorities. Local campaigning is undertaken by IWA's network of branches across the country.

Through its Waterway Recovery Group, IWA works with canal restoration trusts around the country, providing a volunteer workforce, expert engineering and planning advice and information on how to raise the necessary funds. Over 500 miles of canal have been restored and put back to water in the course of IWA's history, with many more currently undergoing restoration.

In this region the IWA is represented by the Peterborough and Great Ouse Branches. Both meet regularly, and welcome new members. To learn more about the IWA's illustrious history, current campaigns, or to find out some of the many benefits of membership, please visit www.waterways.org.uk. The site will also give you up to date contact details for your local branches.

Introduction

Entering the Middle Level

- You will be required to show or purchase a **valid registration (licence) for the Middle Level** *(see p. 17)*
- You will need to demonstrate you have a **current boat safety certificate** and **valid insurance**
- You may be given the free booklet *Middle Level Navigation Notes*
- You will have the opportunity to buy the **non-standard windlass** (1⅜" square (nominal 34mm) required to operate **Ashline**, **Marmont Priory** and **Lodes End locks**
- You will have the opportunity to buy a **key for the March sanitation station** and **Ashline** and **Lodes End Lock security compounds**. Also available from **Middle Level Offices**, **Fox Narrowboats** and **Bill Fen Marina**

At Stanground

This crossing is non tidal. Stanground operates as a sluice as well as a lock, supplying a significant part of the Middle Level's water during low rainfall periods. Never enter the lock without the permission of the lock keeper, and only in their presence. The lock cannot be self-operated.

The lock keeper, Tina, requires 24 hours notice of a crossing ☎ 07824 600470. Should you get an answerphone, leave a message and you will shortly receive a call back.

At Salter's Lode

Crossing on or off the Level requires a short tidal, or estuary, crossing of approximately half a mile between Salter's Lode Lock on the Middle Level and Denver Sluice on the River Great Ouse. This is generally made close to either high tide, or low tide (when the tidal flow is least).

Phone the lock keeper in advance to obtain that day's crossing times. The lock cannot be self-operated. Like all estuary crossings, it can only be undertaken at specific tidal conditions. You can't just turn up and expect to go through.

If you are travelling from Salter's Lode to Denver, ring the Salter's Lode lock keeper, Paul, ☎ 01366 382292. In the reverse direction, Denver to Salter's Lode, call Ben or Dan on ☎ 01366 382340.

Estuary crossings are by definition 'tidal' and should be treated with respect, and demand consideration and preparation. This doesn't mean that they're not fun, so please don't be put off by the following checklists – just stick to them!

Preparation for the estuary crossing

- Avoid undertaking the crossing single handed if at all possible

- Check your boat's insurance covers you for tidal waters

- Check the weather forecast and talk to the lock keeper. If it is too windy, postpone your crossing

- Ensure you've got a reasonable level of fuel. Rougher tidal waters can shake up sediment in the bottom of the tank, so being at least half full is a good idea

- Tidal waters generate strong currents so check your propellor is clear from weed (allowing your prop to operate at maximum efficiency)

- If you've just checked your propellor, now check your weed hatch is securely refastened before you close your engine hatch – undertake a visual check by running your engine in both forward and reverse for short vigorous bursts while still moored

- Check your anchor is available for immediate deployment (not buried at the bottom of a hatch)

- Ensure you have sufficient life jackets for all on board, and wear them!

- Make sure your mobile phone is charged (for communicating with lock keepers) and that you have contact phone numbers for both Lock Keepers

- If you are undertaking a crossing at low tide, have a look at the tidal side of the lock, and note any sandbanks

- Undertake anti bio-contamination measures to prevent the spread of invasive species as necessary

- Always seek the Lock Keeper's advice.

When crossing the estuary

- Ensure everybody on the boat is wearing a life jacket

- Keep pets inside the boat cabin

- Understand whether the tide is coming in or going out

- Follow any advice the Lock Keepers may have given you

- Don't be tempted to cut corners at the lock entrance, there may be a sandbank just below the surface

- Travel with sufficient, but not excessive, engine revs

- Post a look out in the bows to watch for floating debris

- If something unexpected happens, react calmly (don't panic!)

- If you become unable to control your vessel, drop anchor and alert the Lock Keeper

- If you do 'ground' on a sand bank, wait patiently for the tide to lift you off it.

Before you enter the level from the River Nene

Last overnight moorings:
Peterborough Embankment (ample)

Last diesel:
Peterborough Boating Centre
(Stanground Arm – may need to phone
for service ☎ 01733 566688)

Last pump out / water / elsan disposal:
Peterborough Embankment

Last supermarket:
Peterborough (range inc Asda, Co-op,
Morrisons, Sainsbury's, Tesco, Waitrose)

Finding Stanground Lock

Stanground Lock is located off the River
Nene in Peterborough, down the Back
River (some times known as Stanground
Creek). This is a turning on your right
hand side (travelling downstream),
located immediately after you've passed
under the high concrete bridge which
carries the A1139. You pass under a low
railway bridge, and travel 0·75 mile to
Stanground Lock, passing on your way
the rear entrance to the The Woolpack
public house, PE2 8HR ☎ 01733 753544
and **Peterborough Boating Centre**
☎ 01733 566688 which offers a last
chance to buy diesel and some other
chandlery before entering the Level.
Stanground Lock also acts as a sluice,
supplying water to the Middle Level
from the River Nene. It is an attended
lock and should never be entered
without the Lock Keeper being present,
or without their permission. 24 hours
notice is required to make passage
☎ 07824 600470.

Stanground Lock is your opportunity to
acquire the special windlass (see p.24)

necessary for Ashline and Marmont
Priory Locks, the Yale type key
necessary to access Ashline Lock, Lodes
End Lock, and March sanitary station,
and to obtain a copy of the Middle Level
Navigation Notes. It is also the point
from which you will need to display a
valid registration for the Middle Level.

The lock moorings both above and
below the lock are fairly short and only
accommodate one large boat, and you
should be prepared to 'breast up' (moor
alongside another boat) or 'tread water'
while you wait.

Although appearing quite wide, the lock
won't accommodate two boats side by
side. The bottom of the lock is vaulted,
and deeper boats may be instructed to
keep to the middle.

Before you enter the level from the River Great Ouse

Last overnight moorings:
Denver Complex (ample)

Last diesel:
Brandon Creek, PE38 0PR
☎ 07713 465791
info@littleousemoorings.co.uk
(closed Sun, Mon, Tue)

Last pump out / water / elsan disposal:
Denver Complex (around the corner
from the lock, near A G Wright Sluice)
may require EA token

Last supermarket:
Ely (range including Aldi, Iceland,
Sainsbury's, Tesco, Waitrose)

Littleport: Co-op

Downham Market on the relief
channel: Morrison's and Tesco

New Services planned for the Middle Level

The Middle Level Commissioners are planning to build service facilities at both points of entry, Stanground and Salter's Lode. These will be close to the existing facilities off the Level (Peterborough and Denver - see left).

Key to map symbols

	Navigation Authority moorings (EA/MLC)		Foot bridge
	Town and Borough Council moorings		Drinking water
	Marina berths		Chemical disposal point
	Private or permissive moorings		Toilet pumpout
	Boat club moorings		Fuel
	Lock		Public house
	Weir		Railway station
	Winding hole		Church
	Power cable		Supermarket
	Long distance footpath	M	Museum
	Farm bridge		Nature Reserve

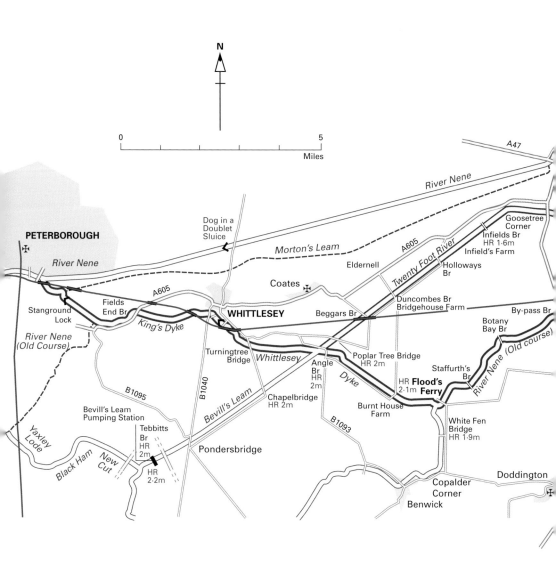

N

0   5
Miles

A47

River Nene

Dog in a
Doublet
Sluice

Morton's Leam

Goosetree
Corner
Infields Br
HR 1·6m
Infield's Farm

A605

Twenty Foot River

Eldernell

Holloways
Br

PETERBOROUGH

River Nene

Coates

Duncombes Br
Bridgehouse Farm

By-pass Br

Fields
End Br

A605

WHITTLESEY

Beggars Br

Botany
Bay Br

Stanground
Lock

King's Dyke

River Nene
(Old Course)

Turningtree
Bridge

Whittlesey

Poplar Tree Bridge
HR 2m

Staffurth's
Br

River Nene (Old course)

Angle
Br
HR
2m

Dyke

HR **Flood's**
2·1m **Ferry**

B1095

B1040

Bevill's Leam

Chapelbridge
HR 2m

Burnt House
Farm

White Fen
Bridge
HR 1·9m

Bevill's Leam
Pumping Station

Tebbitts
Br
HR
2m

Pondersbridge

B1093

Yaxley
Lode

Black Ham

New
Cut

HR
2·2m

Doddington

Copalder
Corner
Benwick

1 MIDDLE LEVEL LINK ROUTE: RIVER NENE TO RIVER GREAT OUSE

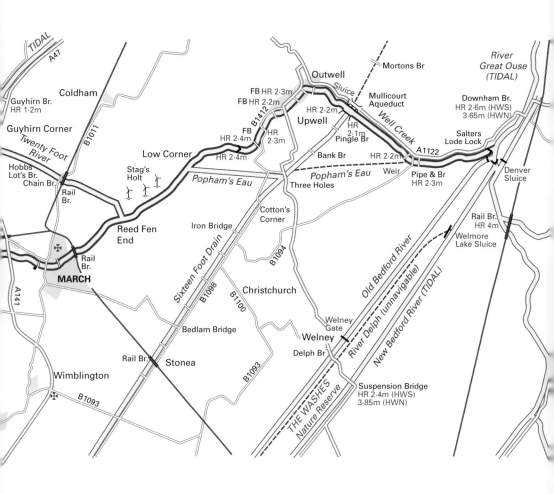

1

MIDDLE LEVEL LINK ROUTE RIVER NENE TO RIVER GREAT OUSE

The recommended Link Route for those who solely wish to transit between the two rivers is between **Stanground Lock** (Peterborough) to **Salter's Lode** (on the estuary of the Great Ouse). This is 28 miles (46km) long and takes on average 9–10 hours. This chapter describes the Link Route, however this guide extends to include a further 100 miles of other waterways on the Middle Level, which amply reward the visitor *(see Chapters 2 and 3 for details)*.

The Middle Level mainly operates at two heights in relation to mean sea level. After entering at either **Stanground** or **Salter's Lode,** you drop to the lower level at either **Ashline** or **Marmont Priory Lock** respectively. This lower level is below mean sea level. The draining of the Fens caused the land to drop as it dried out. In the mid-nineteenth century this middle section was created when the water level was lowered.

> For further information on adjacent waterways, see guides:
> *The River Nene*
> *The River Great Ouse and Tributaries*
> www.imray.com

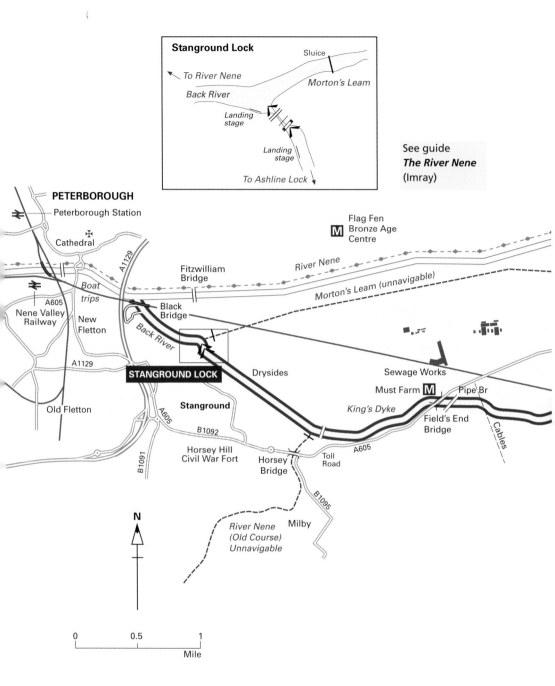

Stanground Lock

To River Nene ←

Sluice

Morton's Leam

Back River

Landing stage

Landing stage

To Ashline Lock ↓

See guide
The River Nene
(Imray)

PETERBOROUGH

Peterborough Station

Cathedral

A1129

Boat trips

A605

Nene Valley Railway

New Fletton

A1129

Old Fletton

Flag Fen
Ⓜ Bronze Age Centre

River Nene

Fitzwilliam Bridge

Morton's Leam (unnavigable)

Black Bridge

Back River

STANGROUND LOCK

Drysides

Sewage Works

Must Farm Ⓜ

Pipe Br

Stanground

King's Dyke

Field's End Bridge

Cables

B1092

A605

Horsey Hill Civil War Fort

Horsey Bridge

Toll Road

B1091

Milby

B1095

River Nene (Old Course) Unnavigable

N

0   0.5   1
Mile

Stanground to Whittlesey Dyke (Angled Junction) and Bevill's Leam

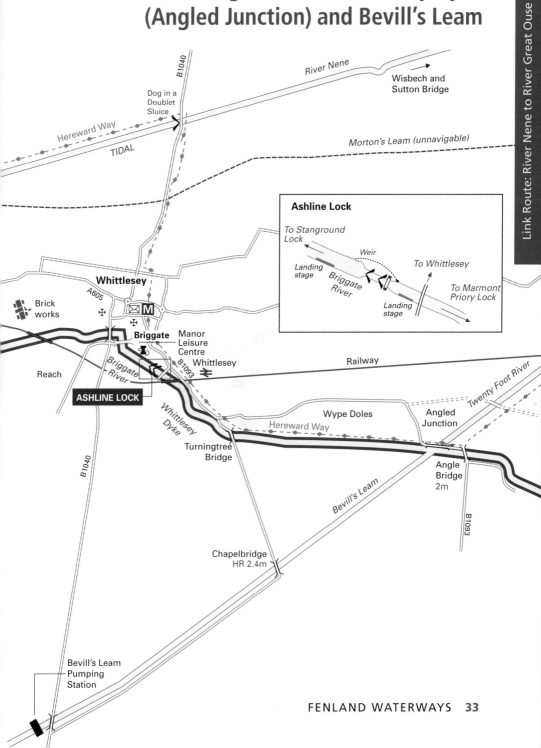

River Nene

Wisbech and
Sutton Bridge

B1040

Dog in a
Doublet
Sluice

Hereward Way

TIDAL

Morton's Leam (unnavigable)

Ashline Lock

To Stanground
Lock

Weir

To Whittlesey

Landing
stage

Briggate
River

To Marmont
Priory Lock

Landing
stage

Whittlesey

A605

Brick
works

Briggate

Manor
Leisure
Centre

Whittlesey

Railway

Briggate
River

B1093

Reach

ASHLINE LOCK

Whittlesey
Dyke

Wype Doles

Hereward Way

Angled
Junction

Twenty Foot River

Turningtree
Bridge

Angle
Bridge
2m

B1040

Bevill's Leam

B1093

Chapelbridge
HR 2.4m

Bevill's Leam
Pumping
Station

Stanground lock

Whittlesey brickworks

Stanground to Whittlesey (Ashline lock)

Approximate travel time 1·5 hours
Distance 4·75 miles

Leaving Stanground Lock, after briefly travelling through a wooded area, which gives way to a housing estate on the righthand (south) bank, you pass a sluice where the course of the **Old River Nene** joins. You are close to the site of **Horsey Hill**, the site of a Civil War fort. Anyone hoping to discern an actual hill may be disappointed. Here in Fenland we measure 'hills' in inches, and in exceptional circumstances, feet. Visitors from more rugged landscapes have been known to fail to even notice a Fenland 'hill'!

The scale of the Fenland landscape now starts to become apparent. This is truly a land of giants! Great pylons march purposefully towards Peterborough, the towering chimneys of Whittlesey brickworks quietly belch smoke, and the landscape is littered with mighty wind turbines, seemingly scratching the sky. After another mile, you will pass under the concrete bridge which carries the evocatively named Milk and Water Drove, where a herd of tower cranes, gathered in a yard, fill the sky.

Here the navigation changes its name from either the River Nene or the Back River, to King's Dyke, so called because it was allegedly dug on the orders of King Canute (*c*.990–1035) to enable trading boats to more easily reach the nearby **Whittlesey Mere** (now drained, *see* The Lost Meres *p.74*).

The old Toll road between Peterborough and Whittlesey (A605) runs next to the navigation for a while. In a lay-by there is a truckers' cafe. The smells of an English breakfast often waft, temptingly, across the water, but there are no easy moorings.

Tower cranes at King's Dyke

The navigation turns under this road and sets off due East. To the north is the Bronze Age site of **Must Farm**. Amongst recent archaeological finds are three bronze age dug out boats, now being stabilised and preserved at the nearby **Flag Fen Archaeology Park**, just two miles north and open to the public.

Flag Fen is another Bronze age site, which appears to have suddenly caught fire and been abandoned, preserving a 'window' into life 3,500 years ago. Sometimes described as 'Britain's Pompeii', it is considered of both national and international significance.

The five chimneys of **Whittlesey brickworks** are now much closer. Lying between the chimneys and King's Dyke are the gargantuan, half-flooded pits where the clay was dug to make bricks. Early this century there was a proposal, now fortunately abandoned, to fill the pits up with London's rubbish!

As you pass under a **railway bridge** the square tower of St Andrew's Church, and the pointed spire of St Mary's, herald your approach into **Whittlesey**. The navigation narrows into a concrete-lined channel and passes under Briggate Bridge before turning abruptly right at the blind 90° **Briggate Bend**.

The Middle Level Commissioners have recently added signage to draw attention to the bend, but it can still 'sneak up' and catch the distracted boater by surprise. The bend will accommodate

Briggate Bridge on the approach into Whittlesey

Moorings and facilities

Overnight moorings at Peterborough Embankment as well as self-operated pump out, water and elsan disposal

48 hour public moorings
Whittlesey, King's Dyke, rear of Manor Leisure Centre, Station Road PE7 1UA

boats up to 70ft. You are advised to send a crew member to the bows, and sound your horn to warn boats travelling in the opposite direction (though I've never actually encountered another boat there). Different people will give you varying advice on how to navigate the bend. Personally I go for 'middle of the stream, at medium pace'. The key consideration to keep in mind is that your boat turns about its centre point.

After another, more comfortable, bend you find the grounds of the **Manor Leisure Centre** on your left.

These are **48 hour public moorings** a short walk from the town centre. Boats sometimes extend the mooring along the bank when the hard moorings are full. Immediately past the moorings is a winding hole, and then **Ashline Lock**.

There are various small shops in **Whittlesey**, including a Co-op, Nisa, Spar

Several pubs are a short walk from the Manor Leisure Centre moorings.
The Black Bull ☎ 01733 203314,
The Falcon Hotel ☎ 01733 351001 and
The Railway Inn ☎ 01733 203555 all serve food.
The George Hotel (Wetherspoons), is less than 5 minutes walk from the leisure centre moorings
☎ 01733 359970

The Boat Inn is a local's waterside pub, but there are no moorings outside
☎ 01733 351668

Places to visit
Whittlesey Museum, Town Hall, Market St, Whittlesey, Peterborough PE7 1BD
www.whittleseymuseum.co.uk

Flag Fen Bronze Age Centre
Flag Fen is well worth a visit if you have time but is a taxi ride away. On the water it is easier to access from the River Nene.
www.vivacity.org/heritage-venues/flag-fen/

Seasonal events
1st Monday in January after Twelfth Night
Plough Monday celebrations, Whittlesey

Fri – Sun 3rd weekend in January -
Whittlesey Straw Bear Festival
www.strawbear.org.uk

Ashline Lock

Whittlesey (Ashline Lock) to March

Approximate travel time 3 hours
Distance 9·5 miles

Ashline Lock

The lock moorings for Ashline (both above and below the lock) are quite short and it may be necessary to be breast up or tread water while you wait. The lock is not wide enough to accommodate two narrowboats side by side. This means that you can't get in (or out) of the lock by opening only one gate and it is absolutely vital to open both gates.

The lock requires the special windlass which you should have purchased, along with a key to access the lock area, on entering the Level (see p. 24). Both top and bottom gates are 'V' style. The sluices can be quite laborious to operate, but always close more easily than they open.

Ashline Lock to Angled Corner

Below the lock the navigation becomes **Whittlesey Dyke.** The banks are now higher and concrete WWII defensive structures, commonly called 'pill boxes' regularly appear bankside (see p.68). Wind turbines populate the horizon in every direction. You pass first industrial buildings, then housing, before you enter the open countryside.

The navigation is intersected at an angle by another channel. To the south west this is **Bevill's Leam,** and to the north east, under the concrete road bridge, is the **Twenty Foot River.**

Off the Link Route:
Angled Junction to Bevill's Leam Pumping Station via Bevill's Leam

Approximate travel time: 1·25 hours
Distance: 4·25 miles (one way)

This is a pretty waterway, quite wide. There isn't a winding point at the end, however the banks are an equal distance apart along the whole waterway. If its not wide enough to turn at the the beginning – don't go any further!

The pumping station is built across the water, preventing navigation further east. A minor road runs alongside for part of the way. Being a dead-end this is one of the very quietest of the Middle Level waterways, and more popular with wildlife than the busier link route.

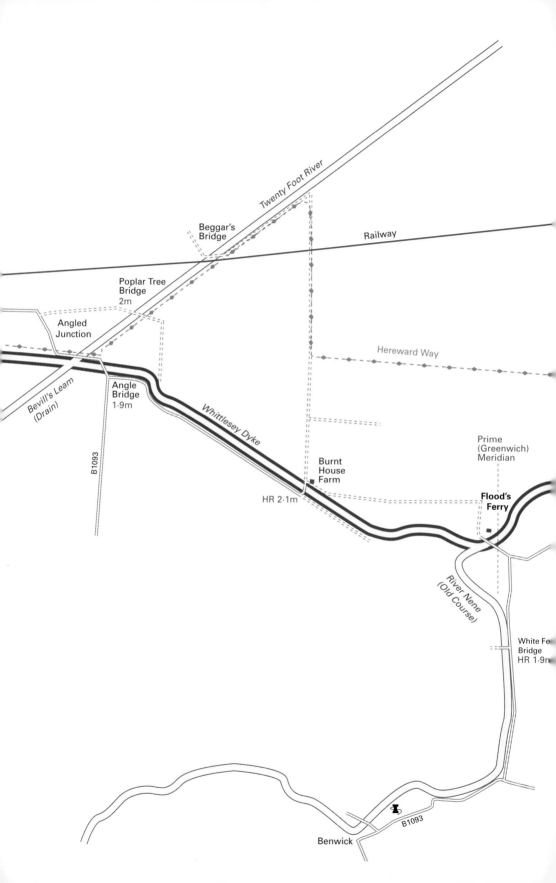

Twenty Foot River

Beggar's
Bridge

Railway

Poplar Tree
Bridge
2m

Angled
Junction

Hereward Way

Bevill's Leam
(Drain)

Angle
Bridge
1·9m

Whittlesey Dyke

B1093

Burnt
House
Farm

Prime
(Greenwich)
Meridian

HR 2·1m

Flood's
Ferry

River Nene
(Old Course)

White Fe
Bridge
HR 1·9n

B1093

Benwick

Whittlesey Dyke (Angle Bridge) to March

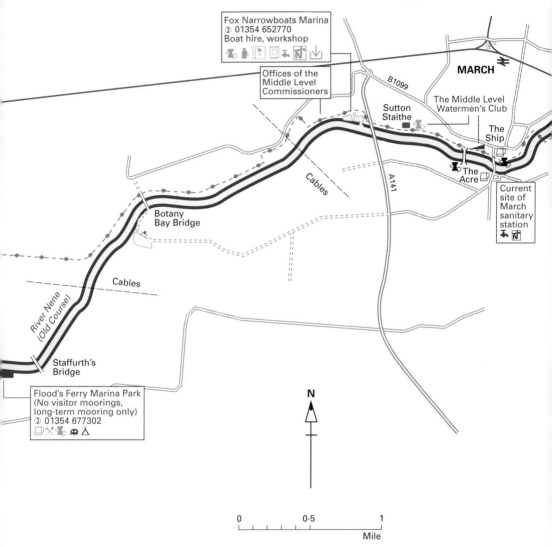

Fox Narrowboats Marina
① 01354 652770
Boat hire, workshop

Offices of the
Middle Level
Commissioners

MARCH

B1099

Sutton
Staithe

The Middle Level
Watermen's Club

The
Ship

The
Acre

A141

Cables

Current
site of
March
sanitary
station

Botany
Bay Bridge

Cables

River Nene
(Old Course)

Staffurth's
Bridge

Flood's Ferry Marina Park
(No visitor moorings,
long-term mooring only)
① 01354 677302

N

0   0·5   1
                         Mile

Angled Junction to Flood's Ferry

From **Angle Bridge**, Whittlesey Dyke eventually joins the Old River Nene at **Flood's Ferry**. Turning to the south leads to **Benwick** (2·5 miles), but the Link Route continues and Whittlesey Dyke continues in a narrow channel for approximately 3·25 miles. Much of it is marked out with fishing 'pegs' with numbers up to 200. Fortunately the author has never seen a match taking place, as the thought of boating through up to 200 anglers is not a pleasant one!

After the bridge you pass the sign indicating the position of the Prime (Greenwich) Meridian. You are now passing from the Western Hemisphere into the Eastern Hemisphere. When crossing the Equator, and moving between the Northern and Southern Hemispheres, it is common practice to perform a ceremony. However no such tradition applies here, as you move from the decadent West into the mystic East!

Middle Level Commissioners offices near March

Moorings and facilities

Flood's Ferry Marina
No visitors' moorings, long term only. Bar, food, slipway, caravans
☎ 01354 677303
www.floodsferry.co.uk

There are **overnight moorings** in **Benwick** (see p.69)

Less than half a mile on, on your right, is **Flood's Ferry Marina Park** which includes long term moorings, holiday cabins and a camp site. Just beyond the marina is **Staffurth's Bridge**.

The river is now much wider although the banks remain comparatively high. An active nature conservation policy by MLC has left fine grasses and reeds lining the river.

At the next bridge the river curves eastwards again. Just as you approach March, the modern offices of the **Middle Level Commissioners** are found on the North bank just before the marina.

The moorings outside the offices of the MLC are intended for their own maintenance craft. Short term mooring is permitted for visitors to the office, but no overnight mooring is allowed.

March to Marmont Priory Lock

Approximate travel time 2 hours
Distance 6·75 miles

Leaving the MLC offices you will pass **Fox Narrowboats Marina** on your left, which offers long and short term moorings, diesel, gas, water and pump-out, chandlery, lift out and marine services.

Passing under the busy A141 you enter the pretty riverside town of **March**. On your left you will pass the **Middle Level Watermens' Clubhouse** *(see p.49)* at **Sutton Staithe**, whilst a few minutes cruising further on, is their slipway with winch at **Skoulding's Rest,** by the green pedestrian **Marylebone Bridge**. On the right hand river bank are **48 hour moorings** provided by the March Town Council. These moorings are the closest to March's largest supermarket, Tesco, which is 1·3 miles away.

A little further on, before the **Town Bridge**, is **March Sanitary Station**. To access it you will need the Yale style key which you bought at either Stanground Lock, or the Offices of the MLC. The pump-out operates on a token. There are outline proposals to relocate March Sanitary Station but the new location is not yet confirmed. There are further moorings opposite, close to the library, public swimming pool and The Acre PH.

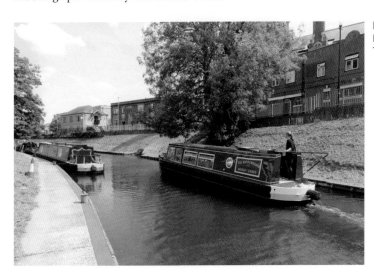

March Town
Moorings outside
The Ship PH

March to Marmont Priory

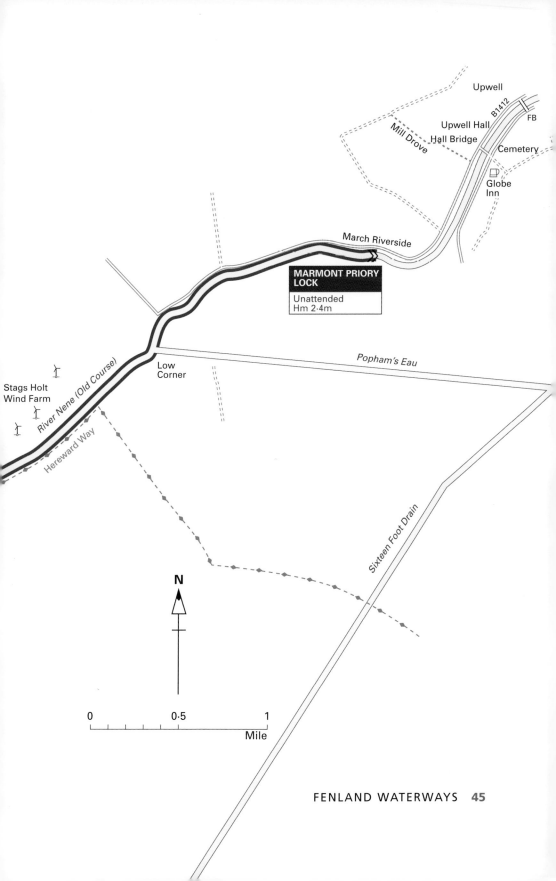

Upwell

B1412

FB

Upwell Hall

Hall Bridge

Cemetery

Mill Drove

Globe Inn

March Riverside

MARMONT PRIORY LOCK

Unattended
Hm 2·4m

Popham's Eau

Low Corner

River Nene (Old Course)

Stags Holt Wind Farm

Hereward Way

Sixteen Foot Drain

N

0   0·5   1
Mile

Just past the Town Bridge are the **Town 48 hour Moorings**. These are in front of The Ship PH, and provide access to town centre shops, a local Wetherspoons and Sainsbury's. They are the best moorings for accessing March railway station (a 20 minute walk).

In the past March has had more than its fair share of neglected and seemingly abandoned boats. This may have been due, in part, to the MLCs previously limited powers of licensing and enforcement, however the Commissioners now have new authority and funding to improve facilities for boaters, and the situation is improving.

Several times I've moored overnight in March, and always been completely comfortable in my surroundings.

March is a popular location for fishing, and there are often fishing competitions, so you need to slow down both as you approach, and pass, fishermen (and women). Passage through March is generally slow because of this and the moored boats which line the banks through much of it, which similarly require moderating your speed and wash. The wooded banks provide natural habitat and the boater is sometimes treated to the electric blue flash of a kingfisher darting along.

Fox Boats

Fox Boats is a family run business, started in 1963 by the enigmatic Charlie Fox. Having initially built himself a wooden sailing dinghy, Charlie progressed to constructing dinghies, fishing boats, and canoes which he hired out. At the same time he worked as retained fireman and taught woodwork part-time at the local grammar school.

In 1973 Charlie was approached by a man with a sketch of a steel cruiser, literally on the back of an envelope. This became the first Fox manufactured steel narrowboat! Inspired, Charlie then built one for his family, then a four boat hire fleet. The rest, as they say, is history!

In 1979 Charlie Fox's business removed to a new marina dug to the west of March.

Sadly, Charlie passed away in 2012, but second and third generations of the family still run the hire fleet, operate the marina, and build an average of two boats a year. Fox boats have a

Fox boat crossing from Denver to Salter's Lode

distinctively cut bow post, raised bows, and are shallow drafted, making them an ideal boat for Fenland waters.

Fox's supports many local water-based clubs and activities, and is an advocate for the local waterways and tourism. Many people's enjoyment of the Fens, over many years, has been from a Fox hire boat.

Moorings and facilities

Fox Narrowboats
Moorings, diesel, gas, pump out, chandlery.
➀ 01354 652770

48hr Town Council moorings on right hand bank after Marylebone Bridge (closest to big supermarkets in March).

48hr Town Council moorings under the Town Bridge, in front of **The Ship** public house.

Moorings opposite March Sanitary Station, close to library, public swimming pool and The Acre public house.

March Sanitary Station at March Town Bridge offers chemical toilet disposal, boat tank flush, potable/drinking water and a boat pump out facility. Key required for access can be bought from MLC ➀ 01354 653232, Fox Narrow Boats, Bill Fen Marina, March library or the Council offices on County Road, or from Stanground, Salter's Lode or Marmont Priory Locks.

Boat hold refuse collection Pump Out facility is token operated. One token costs £13.50 and works for 15 minutes. This gives enough time to empty and flush the tank.

Tokens can be bought from March library or the Council offices on County Road

Middle Level Watermens' Clubhouse
Visitor moorings for small boats are by prior arrangement for Cruising Club members.

March has a Tesco superstore, Sainsbury's, Lidl, Iceland, Cost-Cutter, Co-op, small various other shops
There is a Spar convenience store in **Benwick**

The Ship Inn next to March town quay serves food 01354 607878
The Acre serves food and has moorings ➀ 01354 653203
Ye Olde Griffin serves food, a few minutes walk from town quay
➀ 01354 652517
The Red Lion serves food, close to town quay
➀ 01354 660000
Hippodrome (Wetherspoons) – less than five minutes from town quay
➀ 01354 602980

Places to visit
St Wendreda's Church, 11 Church St, March PE15 9PY

March Museum High St, March PE15 9JJ

RSPB Purl's Bridge Manea, Welches Dam, March PE15 0NF
www.rspb.org.uk/reserves-and-events/reserves-a-z/ouse-washes/

Seasonal events
St George's Day Fayre in March - nearest Saturday to St George's Day
(23rd April)

St Wendreda's Church, March

In the Middle Ages Fenland enjoyed so many religious institutions that it attracted the description the 'Holy Land of the English'. Not all have survived, but the March church of St Wendreda boasts a double hammer beam roof featuring 118 carved angels.

The founder of the Victorian Society, and former Poet Laureate, Sir John Betjeman wrote that the angel roof of St Wendreda's church in March was 'worth cycling forty miles into a head wind' to see.

Those who have braved a fierce Fenland wind blowing from the Urals, uninterrupted by hills or trees, will appreciate quite how much effort is required to cycle so far in these conditions. And those who have visited St Wendreda's will also appreciate quite how well that effort is rewarded – though the roof remains just as spectacular, even if less strenuous means of transport are used when visiting!

On leaving March the wide skies and open country of the Fens embrace you again.

If you are unfortunate enough to have a schedule to adhere to (e.g. getting to Salter's Lode Lock for a crossing at a particular time), you don't need to be too frustrated by having had to slow down through March, because you will have the opportunity 'to catch up on yourself' as the river widens.

Half a mile further on, the **Twenty Foot River** joins on your left. This bypasses March, joining Whittlesey Dyke (Angled Junction) to the River Nene (Old Course) at Reed Fen End *(see p. 50-51)*. As you pass the junction with the Twenty Foot the landscape is dominated by the towering giants of Fenland's largest wind farm which borders the river at Stags Holt.

Just under two miles further along the Old River Nene, **Popham's Eau** departs on your right, taking most of the volume of water with it. You continue a further 1·5 miles along Old River Nene to **Marmont Priory Lock**.

Middle Level Watermens' Club

Too few boaters on the Middle Level appreciate what a debt of gratitude we all owe to the Middle Level Watermens' Club.

By the 1960s commercial traffic on the Middle Level had almost completely dried up, and there was concern that navigation would finish altogether.

In 1963 the Club was formed to fight to save navigation. As Brian Gowler, one of the founding members, explained 'Those boating the Middle Level today sometimes complain of narrow or weedy waterways but few have any idea of the situation …. when M.L.W.C. was formed. Since those days the Sixteen Foot, Twenty Foot, Forty Foot, Reed Fen, Pophams Eau, Bevill's Leam and other sections of the navigation have almost doubled in width and depth'.

Brian recounts, 'On my first trip to Northampton in July 1963, it was necessary to bow haul my boat from Ashline Lock to Stanground taking 12 hours'.

The Club's first President was Teddy Edwards, an early member of the IWA (membership No.14), Secretary to the East Anglian Waterways Association, author of *The Inland Waterways Of Great Britain*, and the leading light in the successful campaign to restore navigation to the Old West River (Great Ouse).

The new club busied itself with providing Club facilities, started cutting back trees across the Level, built landing stages at locks, erected signage, and crucially held annual rallies to attract boaters onto the Level. Most important, they cruised over as wide an area as possible, proving that if they could reach those 'distant' locations, boaters there could reach the market town of March, on the Middle Level.

Many historic victories have been won, the Middle Level is now far more accessible than it ever was, Well Creek has been saved and restored, the Link Route between the Rivers Nene and Great Ouse created, and navigation on the Great Ouse restored all the way up to Bedford.

A small and friendly boaters' association, the Middle Level Watermens' Club has 'punched above its weight' for many years and has much to be proud about!

Stags Holt wind farm

Alternative route (not via March)
Angled Junction to Reed Fen End via Twenty Foot River

Approximate travel time 3 hours
Distance 10·5 miles

Caution: Low bridges

Because of the extremely low bridge heights serious consideration should be given before navigating the Twenty Foot.

The established Link Route includes a section from the Angled Junction on Whittlesey Dyke, north on the River Nene (Old Course) at Floods Ferry, through March and past the junction with the Twenty Foot, north east of March at Reed Fen End. This section of the Link Route represents a journey of 10·5 miles.

Infield's Bridge

There is no suggestion that any boater would want to miss March, but an alternative is to turn left (north east) at the **Angled Junction** on **Whittlesey Dyke** and travel up the **Twenty Foot River** to its northern junction with the **River Nene (Old Course)** north east of **March** at **Reed Fen End**. The journey is almost exactly the same distance as the Link Route, but potentially quicker because it avoids the need to slow down for several miles through March because of moored boats and fishermen.

However, on the **Twenty Foot** you will immediately pass under a **low bridge carrying the B1093**. You are strongly advised to pay specific attention to how much clearance there is between the top of your boat and the bottom of the bridge, as 5 miles further along the Twenty Foot you will encounter **Infields Bridge**. Infields Bridge is is 1'3" (350mm) lower than that first road bridge at the junction.

A veteran boatman tells the story of once arriving at Infields Bridge and finding his boat couldn't pass

Shepperson's Bridge

underneath. He knew a family that lived nearby and knocked on their door for help. Three generations, from Grandfather through to babe-in-arms left the house, trooped down and got on the boat. The vessel, now sitting lower in the water, squeezed under the bridge; then all his guests got off again and returned home!

Remember – if you're too high to get under, and can't recruit temporary extra ballast – it's 5 miles back in the direction you've just come from. Any potential time-saving will have been lost.

Half a mile after **Infields Bridge** the navigation turns east, and after passing under the **A141 Hobbs' Lot Bridge**, passes under an **old railway bridge** which carried the March to Wisbech railway. Called the Bramley line, sadly it

closed to passengers in 1968, and to freight in 2000, but there is a campaign to restore it.

A mile further on the Twenty Foot passes under and chain bridge and a farm bridge. Another mile and you pass under Shepperson's Bridge where the navigation turns again before joining the **River Nene (Old Course)** about half a mile later.

Angled Junction to Reed Fen End via Twenty Foot River

See *guide*
The River Nene
(Imray)

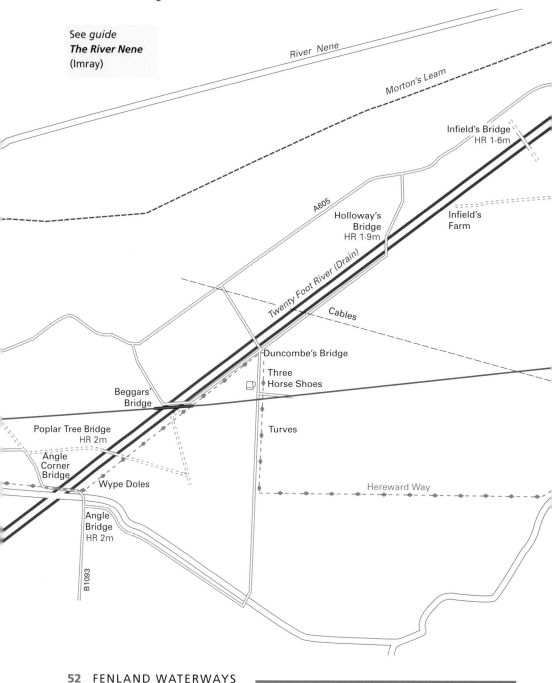

River Nene

Morton's Leam

Infield's Bridge
HR 1·6m

A605

Holloway's
Bridge
HR 1·9m

Infield's
Farm

Twenty Foot River (Drain)

Cables

Duncombe's Bridge

Three
Horse Shoes

Beggars'
Bridge

Poplar Tree Bridge
HR 2m

Turves

Angle
Corner
Bridge

Wype Doles

Hereward Way

Angle
Bridge
HR 2m

B1093

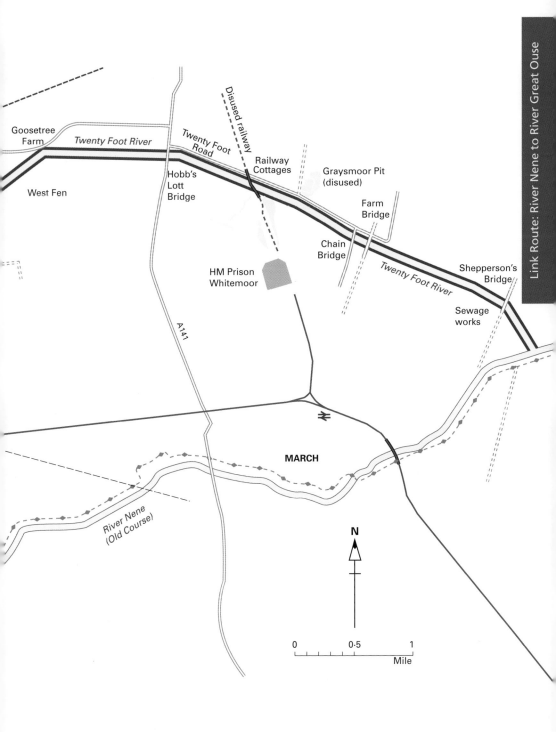

Goosetree
Farm

Twenty Foot River

Twenty Foot
Road

Disused railway

Railway
Cottages

Graysmoor Pit
(disused)

Hobb's
Lott
Bridge

West Fen

Farm
Bridge

Chain
Bridge

Twenty Foot River

Shepperson's
Bridge

HM Prison
Whitemoor

A141

Sewage
works

MARCH

River Nene
(Old Course)

N

0   0·5   1
                Mile

Marmont Priory Lock to Salter's Lode Lock

Approximate travel time 2 hours
Distance 7·5 miles

Marmont Priory Lock is an attended lock. It is important that you ensure all paddles are properly closed as you leave, so as not to accidentally drain Well Creek.

Leaving Marmont Priory Lock you are now on **Well Creek**, and almost immediately you enter the pretty village of **Upwell**. The navigation winds its way through the heart of the village. The spring display of daffodils is always spectacular. Sadly a main road (the A1101) thunders parallel to the Creek, but the architecture is spectacular. Upwell clearly only had a passing acquaintance with the second half of the

The Five Bells pub and St Peter's Church in Upwell

Twentieth Century and 18th and 19th-century buildings have survived in abundance. In parts it is easier to imagine that one is in the Netherlands than England!

Upwell includes St Peter's Church, largely built in the Perpendicular style, which reflects Upwell's considerable former mercantile prosperity. **The Well Creek Trust** *(see p. 58)* provide visitor moorings with a water point. Upwell almost imperceptibly runs into its equally picturesque partner **Outwell**. Despite regular dredging, the narrow connection between the two can be quite shallow (as you pass the British Legion beside the footbridge). However much

Marmont Priory Lock

Moorings

Outwell Basin - Well Creek Trust
provide visitors moorings with a
water point outside St Peter's
church in Upwell on Well Creek.
You can obtain the key to the
water point on the moorings from
the Five Bells pub for a small fee.

Pub moorings
In **Upwell** at the **Globe Inn** and
the **Five Bells** (closed August 2020
so check in advance)
The Crown Lodge Hotel in Outwell
has limited customer moorings for
cruisers immediately outside
The are also moorings outside the
The Crown PH

Upwell has a Post Office, butchers on Town
Street, convenience store, chemist

Several **pubs in Upwell**
The Globe Inn, 1 School Rd, PE14 9EW
☎ 01945 773786
The **Five Bells** (closed August 2020)
1 New Rd, Upwell, Wisbech PE14 9AA
☎ 01945 772222

Outwell has two convenience stores, a chip
shop both a short walk from moorings in the
basin

The Crown Lodge Hotel in **Outwell** has a
restaurant with limited moorings
☎ 07345 773391

The Crown in **Outwell** village, moorings
outside and a popular chip shop (Stott's)
opposite the pub ☎ 01945 773648

Seasonal Events
Last Saturday in May, **Well Creek Trust Raft
Race** in Upwell and Outwell

you 'gun' your engine, you will never
travel any faster down this section, so
the recommendation is to proceed in a
calm and peaceful manner.

Like Upwell, Outwell suffers from the
intrusion of the A1101. We should all be
grateful to the heroic struggles of the
Well Creek Trust, who in the 1970s
fought against the filling in of the Creek
and to preserve navigation. Without
them one can only assume that the road
would have taken over the course of the
Creek, totally dominating the villages,
and probably completely dividing them.

Outwell basin lies at the termination of
the former **Wisbech Canal** (see p. 62),
which was also served by the former
Wisbech and Upwell Tramway (see
p.63). A post nearby commemorates the
Tramway. There are moorings in the
basin.

Parts of the Grade I listed Church of
St Clements date back to the 12th
Century and the church features
intricate 15th-century carvings of
apostles and demons.

Outwell boasts a chip shop, a pub, a
restaurant and two convenience stores.

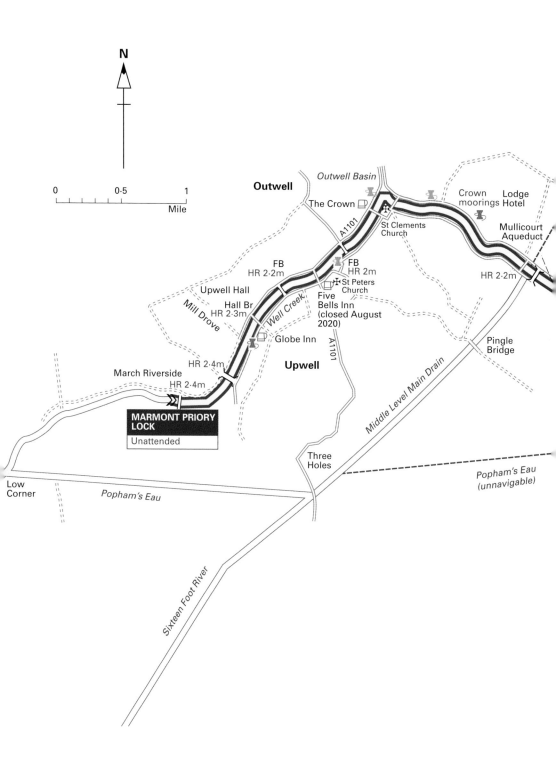

N

0   0·5   1
Mile

Outwell

Outwell Basin

The Crown

Crown moorings   Lodge Hotel

Mullicourt Aqueduct

A1101

St Clements Church

HR 2·2m

FB
HR 2·2m

FB
HR 2m

St Peters Church

Upwell Hall

Mill Drove

Hall Br
HR 2·3m

Well Creek

Five Bells Inn
(closed August 2020)

Globe Inn

A1101

Pingle Bridge

Middle Level Main Drain

HR 2·4m

Upwell

March Riverside
HR 2·4m

MARMONT PRIORY LOCK
Unattended

Three Holes

Popham's Eau (unnavigable)

Low Corner

Popham's Eau

Sixteen Foot River

Marmont Priory Lock to Salter's Lode Lock

Morton's Bridge

Well Creek

A1122 Wisbech Road

Gladys Dack's Cottage

HR 2·2m

Nordelph

A1122

Sluice

Pipe and Bridge 2·3m

Birchfield Road

B1094

Cables

Old Bedford River

Well Creek

Downham West

SALTER'S LODE LOCK
① 01366 382292
Manned, crossings only at specific times
Length 24·4m
Width 3·8m
Head 2·42m

Old Bedford Sluice

Great Ouse

Black Bank Dyke

Relief Channel

AG Wright Sluice

Sluice Road

Downham Market 3 miles

Cut-off Channel

Jenyns Arms

EA 48hr

Denver Sluice

New Bedford River or Hundred Foot Drain (tidal)

See plan p.98

River Wissey

Ten Mile/Ely Ouse

See guide
The River Great Ouse and Tributaries
(Imray)

Well Creek Trust

The Well Creek is an eight mile canalised river which runs between Marmont Priory and Salter's Lode. It has a noble history. Probably used by the Romans, it was definitely employed to move Barnack Stone from Northamptonshire to Ely for the construction of Ely Cathedral. Nowadays it forms part of the only inland link between the rivers Nene and Great Ouse.

King Canute (990–1035) was regularly rowed down it, travelling between Whittlesey and Ely. Once, when the river was frozen, he made the journey by sled.

The Well Creek falls under the jurisdiction of the Middle Level Commissioners. During the 1960s some of the Commissioners argued that the waterway played little part in drainage, and as navigation didn't then bring in any income, could reasonably be filled in, just as the Wisbech Canal had.

In 1969 Norfolk County Council announced plans to widen the Downham Market to Nordelph road (A1122) by filling in the the Creek. A protest meeting was held, and a Public Inquiry in September 1969 recommended that 'the Well Creek must not be closed'.

The Well Creek Trust was formed in May 1970 to save, and re-open the Creek. After Herculean efforts by a task-force, which included the Trust, the Middle Level Watermens' Club, the Cambridge Branch of the IWA Waterway's Recovery Group, the Army Cadet Force, and the local WI, navigation was restored in 1975.

In conjunction with the MLC the Trust has constructed, and now maintains, moorings at Upwell (outside the Church), Outwell (in the basin), Barrow Dale Grove, Nordelph (Gladys Dack's) and at Salter's Lode. They are also to be thanked for the annual display of spring flowers.

The Trust raises funds to maintain the Creek and moorings and holds a raft race / fun day every year around the last Saturday in May. The MLC maintain the right to close the Creek for skating. But sadly recent winters have been too warm for this to take place.

Anyone using the Well Creek owes a considerable debt of gratitude to the Trust and its members who fought so hard, in the face of what may sometimes have appeared insurmountable odds, to save and re-open this important waterway. Since the Middle Level Act became law in November 2018, the Commissioners have been granted powers to charge for navigation on the Level. This should relieve the necessity for the Trust to raise funds to maintain a waterway which we all enjoy.

www.wellcreektrust.org.uk

Just after the basin there is a large brick built commercial quay which is further testimony to the once high level of trade along Well Creek. Sadly there is not mooring access to the convenience store (which doubles as a kebab shop) facing it.

On leaving Outwell you cross the **Sixteen Foot Drain** (as it becomes the **Middle Level Main Drain**) on **Mullicourt Aqueduct**. The A1122 runs alongside the navigation but as you leave the straggling houses behind, the road is partly shielded by a bank. **Gladys Dack's moorings** are remote but although flanked by the road can be surprisingly peaceful, depending on the wind direction.

Gladys Dack's Public Staithe

Gladys Dack's Public Staithe provides a pleasant, remote mooring on the North Bank of Well Creek between Mullincourt Aqueduct and Nordelph. But who was the eponymous Gladys Dack whose name is remembered?

Opposite the landing stage, on the South bank of the river, is an old broken-backed ruin gradually disappearing from view behind trees, nettles and brambles. This was home to Gladys Dack, built by her father Frederick. Gladys lived there for almost all her life.

As was commonly the case in the countryside in the first half of the twentieth century, the cottage had no electricity, gas, mains water or mains sewerage. Lighting would have been by candle or paraffin light, cooking on a crude stove or a 'range' fueled by scavenged wood, and water either drawn by pump, or taken straight from the Creek.

Access to the cottage from the road between Outwell and Nordelph (now the A1122) was by crossing the Creek on a plank, which once

used, had to be pulled back to permit boats to pass. The image of the remote and primitive cottage, which could only be reached by a make-shift drawbridge, may sound romantic, but the reality of it is actually quite chilling. The thought of an elderly lady, in winter, crossing the cold waters of the creek on an icy plank, is really quite disturbing!

Gladys is understood to have passed away in the late 1980s, having spent her last few years in a nursing home.

Two miles after crossing Mullicourt Aqueduct you arrive at **Nordelph**. By now even the village names sound Dutch. The navigation bears to the left, near a small weir where **Popham's Eau** used to flow into the Creek. Sadly the village pub closed a few years ago, and there are no shops in Nordelph.

Salter's Lode Lock is not much more than a mile further on from the end of Nordelph.

The navigation is raised above the level of the adjoining road. Once again the

shallow channel defies travelling fast. **Salter's Lode** is only a small hamlet. Downham Market is about 3 miles away, but is an unpleasant walk along a busy road. There are, however a couple of taxi firms in Downham Market and it has a railway station.

Hopefully you will have phoned Paul, (☎ 01366 382292) the Salter's Lode lock-keeper, to find out in advance at what time the tide will be permit the crossing to Denver. Actual tide times don't always adhere to those forecast, so it is a good idea to let Paul know you have

Salter's Lode Lock

arrived, and also to be ready to leave up to quarter of an hour before schedule. Please refer to our crossing guide on pages 24-25.

Leaving Salter's Lode Lock you are entering Environment Agency waters and will need an appropriate EA registration. If you are travelling in the opposite direction, you need to ensure that your EA registration remains valid for the Middle Level. Salter's Lode is your opportunity to obtain a copy of the current Middle Level Navigation Notes and to acquire the special windlass (see p.24) necessary for Ashline and Marmont Priory Locks, the Yale type key necessary to access Ashline Lock, Lodes End Lock, and March Sanitary Station.

For navigation on the River Great Ouse, see
The River Great Ouse and Tributaries
(Imray)
www.imray.com

Moorings and facilities

Gladys Dack's Public Staithe, Nordelph, Well Creek

At **Salter's Lode Lock** acquire special windlass *(see p. 24)* for Ashline and Marmont Priory Lock and Yale type key for Ashline Lock, Lodes End Lock and March Sanitary Station
☎ 01366 382292

Overnight moorings at Salter's Lode, Well Creek

The Jenyns Arms
Geographically the nearest pub is the Jenyns Arms, about 0·25 miles away from Salter's Lode as the crow flies. However there is no bridge across the intervening New Bedford River. Unless you fancy a dip (strongly not recommended) the journey by road is 5 miles! It is the only pub in the country owned by the Environment Agency.

For more infomation on Downham Market see *The River Great Ouse* (Imray).

Well Creek and the King's lost treasure

The comic history book *1066 And All That* says of King John (1166–1216) that he 'begun badly as a Bad Prince', and 'finally demonstrated his utter incompetence by losing the Crown and all his clothes in the wash'. Of course this isn't an accurate historic account, but it is generally agreed that John did lose the Crown Jewels to the waters somewhere around here.

The earliest chronicler of the events, shortly after Magna Carta, was Roger of Wendover (died 1236), a Benedictine monk at St Albans Abbey. He gives a graphic account of King John's journey from King's Lynn to Wisbech, suggesting that the king's belongings, including the Crown Jewels, were lost as he crossed one of the tidal estuaries which empties into the Wash, being sucked in by quicksand and whirlpools.

Another report stated: 'Then, journeying towards the north, in the river which is called Wellstream, by an unexpected accident he lost all his wagons, cars and sumpter horses with the treasures, precious vessels and all the other things which he loved so well; for the ground was opened up in the middle of the waves, and bottomless whirlpools swallowed them all up'.

The Welle Stream was also known as the 'Welnye' 'Old Wellenhee', or 'Old Croft River'. Where is, or was, the Welle Stream? The routes of the rivers Nene and Ouse were significantly different, before everything changed almost beyond recognition by Cornelius Vermuyden's great drainage works in the 17th century.

But the Welle Stream still exists in Upwell and Outwell, part of the same Welle Stream in which King John lost his treasure crossing! So when you cruise along Well Creek cast your eyes downwards into the waters. King John's fabled lost treasure just might be waiting nearby for you to find it!

Wisbech Canal

In the late 18th century Wisbech, fearing its prosperity was being threatened by the growth of King's Lynn, resolved to strengthen its trade links by the construction of a canal between the River Nene in Wisbech and the Well Creek in Outwell.

Opened 1796, the canal largely followed the line of the Old Welle Stream an important river from the pre Vermuyden era. It was a level canal with the only locks being at either end. It was fed from the Nene by opening the gates and allowing water in at High Tide on Spring Tides. These tides inevitably carried and deposited silt. For its entire, short, life the canal suffered from silting up, and water shortages because it could only be filled fortnightly.

Although primarily carrying freight, a passenger service ran for a few years – Whybrow's packet, which charged 2d from Outwell to Wisbech. The passenger service ceased with the opening of the Wisbech and Upwell Steam Tramway in 1883.

In 1926 a Warrant of Abandonment was issued on the canal, and it closed. During the 1960s it was filled in.

Wisbech and Upwell Tramway

The Wisbech & Upwell Tramway played a surprisingly important part in the changing history of 19th and 20th-century transport.

The tramway was built in 1883–4 to compete with the Wisbech Canal. The authorisation to construct it was contained in the 1881 Great Eastern Railway Act. To save costs it was constructed under the Tramway Act of 1870. The track was laid to the standard railway specification rather than the alternative tramway spec. It served Wisbech, Outwell and Upwell, for the most part running next to Well Creek and the Wisbech Canal.

The line was popular from the outset, with 3,000 passengers a week using it in 1884. This success led to the passing of the 1896 Light Railways Act which resulted in the construction of many more localised light railways around the country. The initial speed limit of 8mph, was raised to 12mph in 1904.

The Wisbech canal was already struggling when the tramway opened, and it gradually lost more and more trade to the tramway, eventually closing in 1922. However, by then the tramway was itself facing increasing competition from road transport – specifically buses – and the passenger service finished in 1927. The tramway coaches transferred to other light railways, with one coach appearing in the classic 1953 Ealing film *The Titfield Thunderbolt*.

Freight traffic continued on the tramway. Its original steam engines were replaced by diesel and in 1952 it achieved the dubious distinction of being the first line in Britain to be entirely powered by diesel locomotives. Sadly, in 1966 the line fell victim to the Beeching Act, finally closing on 23 May 1966.

The Rev. W. Awdry was fan of the tramway, and in his book *Toby the Tram Engine*, Toby, and his coach Henrietta are based on stock used on the line.

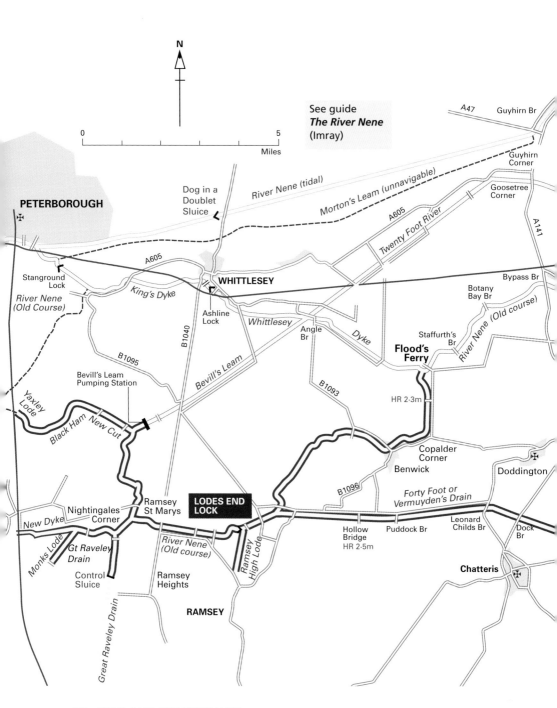

N

0   5
Miles

See guide
The River Nene
(Imray)

A47   Guyhirn Br

Guyhirn
Corner

River Nene (tidal)

Morton's Leam (unnavigable)

Dog in a
Doublet
Sluice

PETERBOROUGH

A605

Goosetree
Corner

Twenty Foot River

A141

A605

WHITTLESEY

Stanground
Lock

King's Dyke

River Nene
(Old Course)

Ashline
Lock

B1040

Whittlesey

Dyke

Angle
Br

Bypass Br

Botany
Bay Br

Staffurth's
Br

River Nene (Old course)

Flood's
Ferry

B1095

Bevill's Leam

B1093

HR 2·3m

Bevill's Leam
Pumping Station

Yaxley
Lode

Black Ham   New Cut

Copalder
Corner

Benwick

Doddington

B1096

Forty Foot or
Vermuyden's Drain

Ramsey
St Marys

**LODES END
LOCK**

Nightingales
Corner

New Dyke

River Nene
(Old course)

Ramsey High Lode

Hollow
Bridge
HR 2·5m

Puddock Br

Leonard
Childs Br

Dock
Br

Monks Lode

Gt Raveley
Drain

Control
Sluice

Ramsey
Heights

Chatteris

Great Raveley Drain

RAMSEY

2 FLOOD'S FERRY TO POPHAM'S EAU VIA FORTY FOOT AND SIXTEEN FOOT
AND NO-THROUGH WATERWAYS WEST OF WELLS BRIDGE

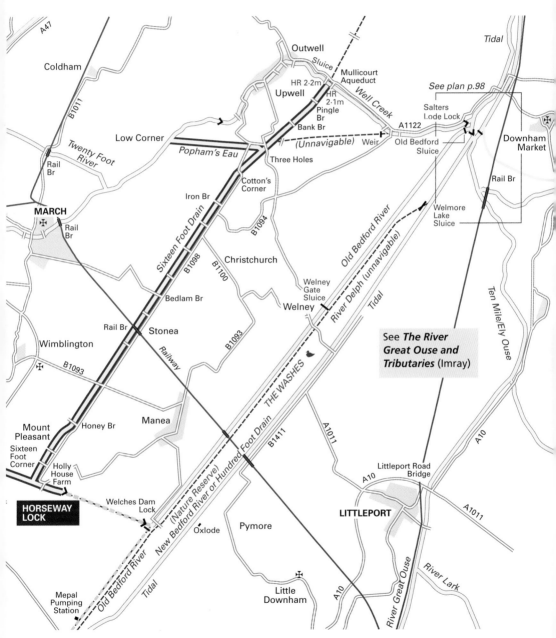

2

ALTERNATIVE ROUTE
FLOOD'S FERRY TO POPHAM'S EAU
VIA FORTY FOOT AND
SIXTEEN FOOT

AND NO-THROUGH WATERWAYS WEST OF WELLS BRIDGE

The main Link Route includes a section detailed in Chapter 1, from Flood's Ferry, through March, and north east to the junction with Popham's Eau. This is a journey of 9·5 miles.

An alternative route covering much more of the Middle Level turns south at at Flood's Ferry and follows the River Nene to its junction with the Forty Foot Drain at Well's Bridge, turning east along the Forty Foot Drain, north up the Sixteen Foot Drain to Popham's Eau at

Three Holes, and then west along Popham's Eau direct to its junction with the River Nene (Old Course). This is a journey of 27 miles.

There is also the option to explore westwards from Well's Bridge. The route to Yaxley Lode is a dead end for navigation but offers an opportunity to visit Ramsey High Lode and other peaceful waters off the beaten track.

River Nene (Old Course)
Floods Ferry to Well's Bridge

Approximate travel time 10·5 hours
Distance 28 miles

Travelling south on the **River Nene (Old Course)** from **Flood's Ferry** it is noticeably narrower, shallower and more meandering than on the main Link Route. Generally this is the case if you compare the navigations in the south west of the Level to those in the north east. Because the Level drains to the north east, all the navigations acquire more water and grow in this direction.

Much of the Middle Level waterways are overlooked by concrete 'pill boxes' – defensive structures surviving from WWII. Nowhere do they appear more frequently than on this section of the Nene.

Some 0·75 of a mile south from Flood's Ferry you encounter **White Fen Farm Bridge**. This is the lowest bridge on the River Nene (Old Course), and is clearly 'flagged-up' as having reduced air clearance.

Pillboxes

The banks of Fenland waters are littered with concrete pillboxes, the River Nene (Old Course) featuring over a dozen. About 26,000 of these defences were hurriedly constructed across Southern England during 1940 after the evacuation of the British Army from Dunkirk, in preparation of an anticipated invasion by the German Army. They feature on the (old) Nene in an unusually high density. They were not built to prevent enemy boats travelling up the rivers, but to turn the rivers themselves into lines of defence. Bridges were mined with explosives and would have been blown up when news of a foreign invasion was received, thus forcing enemy tanks into hazardous river crossings. It remains a sobering thought that it was once anticipated that the front line of WWII might have been formed along these now quiet waters!

Pill box at the junction of Whittlesey Dyke and River Nene (Old Course) near Flood's Ferry

Moorings and facilities

Funded by Peterborough IWA, Benwick Parish Council and the Middle Level Watermens' Club, **Benwick moorings** are just North of the B1093 Whittlesey Road.

The Five All's pub in **Benwick** is visited both by Peterborough Branch IWA and the Middle Level Watermens' Club – so it is guaranteed 'boater friendly'
☎ 01354 677520
Benwick also has a **Spar** convenience store on the High Street.

River Nene (Old Course)

Less than 2 miles further on you reach the pretty village of **Benwick** where old timbers pay testimony to a great wharf that once stood at the side of the river.

Beyond Benwick the river winds through peaceful countryside for another 5 miles before it reaches its junction with the **Forty Foot or Vermuyden's Drain**, just under a concrete road bridge at **Well's Bridge**. Well's Bridge is a small hamlet with little more than a large dealership in motor caravans.

Connected no-through waterways west of Well's Bridge

Well's Bridge to Lodes End Lock

Approximate travel time: 15 minutes
Distance: 0·75 miles

Well's Bridge lies at the junction of the **River Nene (Old Course)** and the **Forty Foot Drain** which heads eastwards.

To the south-west the River Nene (Old Course) continues under two further bridges, **Bodsey Bridge** and **Saunder's Bridge**, to the junction with **Ramsey High Lode**, followed immediately by

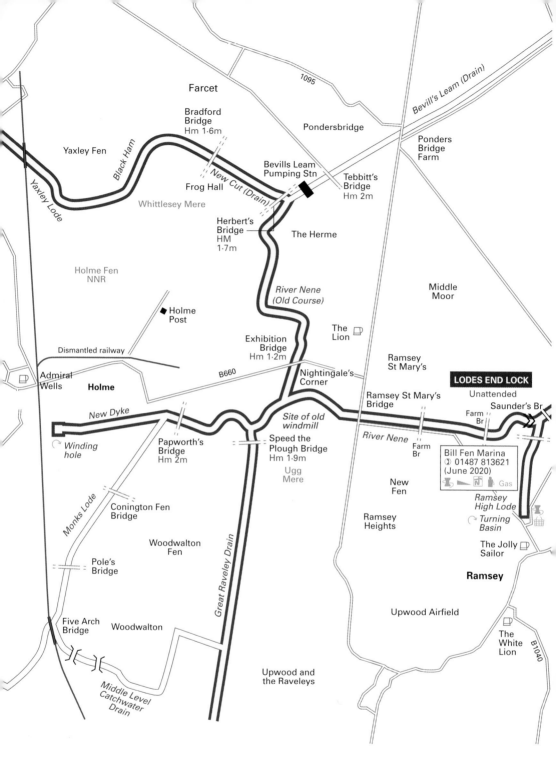

Farcet

Bradford
Bridge
Hm 1·6m

Pondersbridge

Bevill's Leam (Drain)

1095

Ponders
Bridge
Farm

Yaxley Fen

Black Ham

Yaxley Lode

New Cut (Drain)

Frog Hall

Whittlesey Mere

Bevills Leam
Pumping Stn

Tebbitt's
Bridge
Hm 2m

Herbert's
Bridge
HM
1·7m

The Herme

Holme Fen
NNR

Holme
Post

River Nene
(Old Course)

Middle
Moor

Dismantled railway

Admiral
Wells

Holme

B660

Exhibition
Bridge
Hm 1·2m

The
Lion

Nightingale's
Corner

Ramsey
St Mary's

LODES END LOCK

Unattended

Saunder's Br

New Dyke

Winding
hole

Papworth's
Bridge
Hm 2m

Speed the
Plough Bridge
Hm 1·9m

Site of old
windmill

Ugg
Mere

Ramsey St Mary's
Bridge

River Nene

Farm
Br

Farm
Br

Bill Fen Marina
☎ 01487 813621
(June 2020)

Gas

New
Fen

Ramsey
High Lode

Turning
Basin

Monks Lode

Conington Fen
Bridge

Woodwalton
Fen

Pole's
Bridge

Ramsey
Heights

The Jolly
Sailor

Ramsey

Great Raveley Drain

Five Arch
Bridge

Woodwalton

Upwood Airfield

The
White
Lion

B1040

Middle Level
Catchwater
Drain

Upwood and
the Raveleys

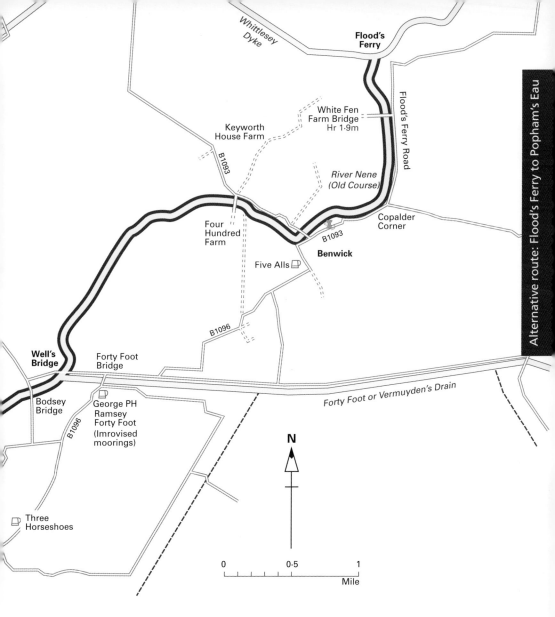

Whittlesey Dyke

Flood's Ferry

Flood's Ferry Road

White Fen Farm Bridge Hr 1·9m

Keyworth House Farm

River Nene (Old Course)

B1093

Copalder Corner

Four Hundred Farm

B1093

Benwick

Five Alls

Well's Bridge

Forty Foot Bridge

B1096

Bodsey Bridge

George PH Ramsey Forty Foot (Imrovised moorings)

B1096

Forty Foot or Vermuyden's Drain

Three Horseshoes

N

0   0·5   1
Mile

River Nene (Old Course)
Floods Ferry to Well's Bridge
(and no-through waterways west of Well's Bridge)

Lodes End Lock which is little more than a stop lock. When the water is at the same level on both sides, and both sets of gates are open, it can be taken 'on the level'.

Ramsey High Lode

About a mile beyond **Well's Bridge** and just before **Lodes End Lock, Ramsey High Lode** is a short channel (only 1 mile long) which leaves the River Nene (Old Course) and travels almost due south, providing access to both **Bill Fen Marina**, and **Ramsey**. The entrance to Bill Fen Marina is on the right just after the footbridge. The turning basin at the far end provides mooring and direct access to Ramsey.

The watercourse used to continue into the centre of Ramsey and along the main street, Great Whyte, which was once an open quay. However, the navigation was built over in 1854 and the water diverted into a tunnel which still runs underneath.

Ramsey

Moorings and facilities

Overnight moorings in the **Ramsey turning basin** at the far end of **Ramsey High Lode**

Bill Fen Marina ☏01487 813621 moorings, diesel, gas, pump out, chandlery (June 2020)

Tesco superstore next to the turning basin, small shops and restaurants in Ramsey

Pubs in Ramsey: **The Jolly Sailor, The Angel, The George Inn**

Fenland Light Railway (miniature steam railway – summer opening) Mereside Drove, Ramsey Mereside, PE26 2UE

Ramsey Rural Museum
Wood Lane, PE26 2XD
www.ramseyruralmuseum.co.uk

Ramsey Walled Kitchen Garden
Wood Lane, PE26 2XD
www.ramseywalledgarden.org

Ruins of Ramsey Abbey (World Heritage Site) Abbey School, PE26 1DH

Ramsey Golf Club
4 Abbey Rooms Ln, PE26 1DD

The Admiral Wells gastro pub in **Holme** is ten minutes walk from the head of Yaxley Lode ☏01487 831214

Holme Post (lowest point in GB - iron post see p. 74) in **Holme Fen National Nature Reserve**
www.greatfen.org.uk/holme-fen

Seasonal events
Ramsey Carnival third Saturday in July
Plough Day and Country Fair,
Ramsey Rural Museum last Sunday of September
Ramsey 1940s Weekend, third weekend in August

Lodes End lock with both gates open at the same time. The lock acts as a stop lock and sometimes the waters are at the same height both sides of the lock.

West of Lodes End Lock

A further 14 miles (approximately) of navigable waterways can be accessed through **Lodes End Lock**, bounded in the west by the main **East Coast railway line**. These remote waterways are beautifully peaceful, full of wildlife, and almost devoid of other boating traffic.

These waters are well worth a leisurely visit and we leave you to explore them for yourselves. In 2017 Peterborough IWA visited these charming waters and mooring near the winding point at the end of New Dyke, from where the Admiral Wells PH at Holme is only a short walk across a couple of fields.

The Great Fen Project

The Great Fen project was started in 2001 with the aim of 'rewilding' a 3,700 hectare wetland connecting Woodwalton Fen with Holme Fen (on the south-western shore of the former Whittlesey Mere). The area was once 'wild fen', a landscape rich in wildlife and diversity, but the draining of the Fens, removal of peat, and intensive modern farming techniques resulted in 99% of the wild fen being destroyed.

This is is a long-term project, of national significance, managed in partnership by the EA, Huntingdonshire DC, the Middle Level Commissioners, Natural England and the Wildlife Trust for Beds, Cambs & Northants. Its patrons have included John Major (former local MP and PM), Tim Smith (Eden Project),

Beth Rothschild and currently Prince Charles. Stephen Fry is president.

Its aim is not to re-flood Whittlesey Mere (drained 1851) or Ugg Mere, but to return the area to natural habitat. In addition to forming the largest Silver Birch woodland in lowland Britain, Holme Fen includes a couple of acres of remnant raised bog, an echo of the habitat that would have dominated the area centuries ago.

The reserve is open to the public throughout the year, with talks, guided walks and other activities taking place at the Countryside Centre in Ramsey Heights.

www.greatfen.org.uk

The Lost Meres

Although much of Fenland had been drained in the 17th century, lakes, locally called Meres, remained as testament to Fenland's waterlogged past. Holme Mere, Ugg Mere, and Trundle Mere were situated respectively near Holme, Ramsey and Yaxley. Whittlesey Mere was the largest lowland lake south of the Lake District with an estimated summer time size of 2,000 acres, growing to 3,000 acres in winter.

All the meres were a valuable source of fish and eels (with the rights owned by local religious houses prior to the dissolution of the monasteries), as well as wild fowling. Whittlesey Mere had been popular for boating, regattas and skating matches in winter (see Fen Skating page 86). In 1697 the traveller Celia Fiennes described it as '3 mile broad and six mile long'.

In 1774 George Walpole, 3rd Earl of Oxford, led an small armada of boats on a pleasure cruise through 'the narrow seas of Cambridgeshire, Lincolnshire, Northamptonshire, Huntingdonshire, and Norfolk'. Their journal records several fun filled days spent on Whittlesey Mere. They took with them a carpenter to demolish bridges which were too low for them to pass underneath, and rebuild once they had got through. Which demonstrates that low bridges aren't just a modern consideration!

At the Great Exhibition of 1851 an innovative Appold centrifugal pump was displayed, which had a far greater capacity than the previous scoop wheel, and its inventor was commissioned to design a great pump to drain Whittlesey Mere.

The Holme Post

All the meres, including Holme Mere were drained. Anticipating the shrinkage of the peat, a cast-iron post, probably originally intended for the Great Exhibition's 'Crystal Palace', was driven completely into the ground at Holme, so that top of the post finished at ground level. As the ground sank, gradually the full post emerged. In addition to the whole of the 12 foot post being exposed, a six foot extension has been added underneath it. Fen folk say that a drained mere will 'shrink by the height of man, in the lifetime of that man'. As a rule of thumb this works pretty well for the Holme Post where the ground has shrunk the height of three men, in three men's lifetimes.

The post and its extension remain to this day. Holme Fen is the lowest point in Britain and nothing demonstrates more vividly how much the drained land has sunk.

The Holme Post after steel guys had been added for support
South Holland DC

Forty Foot Drain:
Well's Bridge to Sixteen Foot Drain

Approximate travel time 3 hours
Distance 8 miles

From **Well's Bridge** turning left (east) onto the **Forty Foot Drain** you leave the world of the winding river and rejoin the world of mechanically straight, wide, man-made navigations. After half a mile mile you pass under the **B1096 road bridge** and immediately to your right, hiding behind a concrete pill box, is **The George at Ramsey Forty-Foot** public house. This attractively located pub has changed hands several times in the last few years but has always welcomed

boaters. There are no hard moorings, but Peterborough IWA have several times moored 'fleets' of up to eight boats bankside.

The Forty Foot continues deadstraight for 2·5 miles, where it kinks slightly between the footbridge and **Puddock Bridge**. It continues straight again to **Leonard Child's Bridge** (locals still call it by its original name, Carter's Bridge). A minor road runs parallel and close to the

'Wild' moorings outside The George at Ramsey Forty-Foot

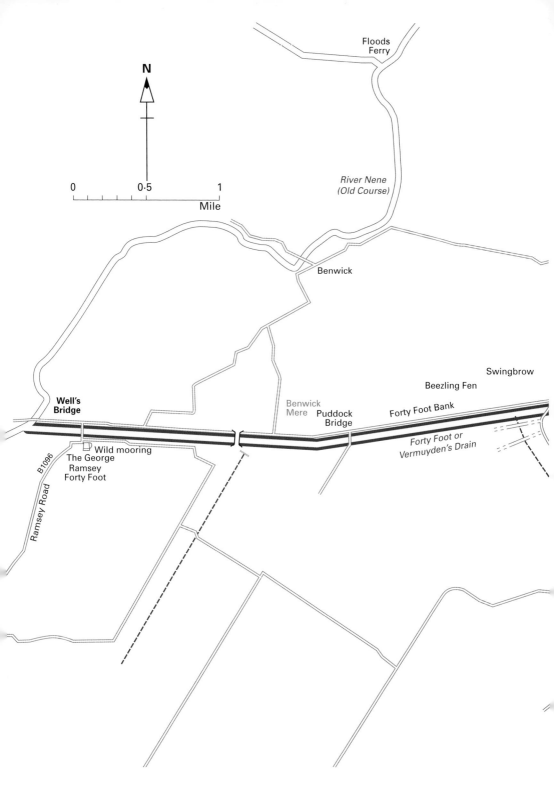

N

0   0.5   1
Mile

Floods
Ferry

River Nene
(Old Course)

Benwick

Swingbrow

Beezling Fen

Well's
Bridge

Forty Foot Bank

Benwick
Mere   Puddock
Bridge

Forty Foot or
Vermuyden's Drain

Wild mooring
The George
Ramsey
Forty Foot

Ramsey Road

B1096

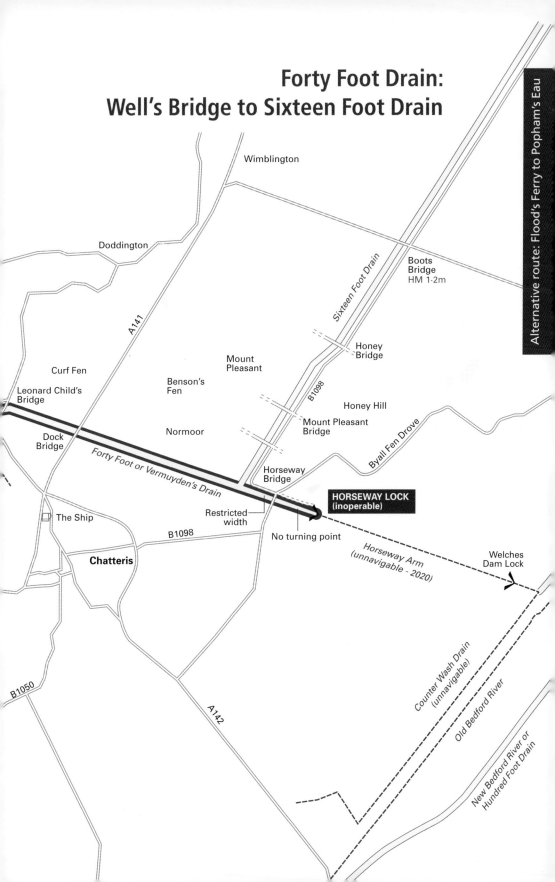

Forty Foot Drain:
Well's Bridge to Sixteen Foot Drain

Alternative route: Flood's Ferry to Popham's Eau

Wimblington

Boots
Bridge
HM 1·2m

Doddington

Sixteen Foot Drain

Honey
Bridge

A141

Mount
Pleasant

Curf Fen

Benson's
Fen

B1098

Honey Hill

Leonard Child's
Bridge

Mount Pleasant
Bridge

Byall Fen Drove

Normoor

Dock
Bridge

Forty Foot or Vermuyden's Drain

Horseway
Bridge

HORSEWAY LOCK
(inoperable)

The Ship

Restricted
width

B1098

No turning point

Horseway Arm
(unnavigable - 2020)

Welches
Dam Lock

Chatteris

B1050

A142

Counter Wash Drain
(unnavigable)

Old Bedford River

New Bedford River or
Hundred Foot Drain

Chatteris Dock c.1903

edge of the bank. Although busy, the road is not particularly noisy, due in part to the installation of average speed cameras in 2010, following a road safety campaign by this author, his wife, and the late Ramsey Councillor Ray Powell.

Passengers and drivers in passing cars often appear pleased to see boats so close-by, and frequently wave. I tend to

keep to the centre of the channel, just in case one of these distracted drivers ends up in the water! This is the through route to Popham's Eau.

After Leonard Child's Bridge the road disappears, whilst the navigation continues in a straight line for another three miles. Just past the **A141 road bridge**, built on the line of the Chatteris to March railway, is the site of the former **Chatteris Dock** to your right. Sadly there is no longer provision for moorings, but Chatteris Town Council hope one day to fix this. On your left you can see the former **Boat PH** which once served thirsty dock workers.

After open country you reach the junction on your left with the **Sixteen Foot Drain** which heads off northeast.

Forty Foot at Well's Bridge

Moorings and facilities

Improvise 'wild' moorings outside **The George** PH at Ramsey Forty-Foot
☏ 01487 290024

Horseway Arm of the Forty Foot Drain

After its junction with the Sixteen Foot Drain, the Forty Foot Drain continues east and is navigable, with some difficulty, for half a mile to **Horseway Lock**. The lock is currently closed because the channel beyond it is out of water and awaiting restoration.

There is no winding point below Horseway Lock and it is too narrow to turn even a forty foot boat.

The Peterborough Branch of the IWA periodically visits Horseway in support of the Project Hereward campaign *(see p. 80)* to re-open navigation through to the Old Bedford River at Welches Dam. They take boats up to Horseway lock in pairs, arranged push-me-pull-you (tied together stern to stern), so that one boat pulls its partner in, and the second boat pulls the first back out again.

They do this early in the season as, not having any throughflow, the channel is prone to weeding in summer.

The dry channel between **Horseway Lock** and **Welches Dam Lock** runs for 2·25 miles. Although unnavigable it is a worthwhile walk.

Push-me-pull-you to the Horseway Lock

Welches Dam Lock

Project Hereward

Hereward the Wake is often called the 'last Englishman'. Following the Norman invasion of England in 1066, Ely was the last area of England to refuse to swear allegiance to William the Conqueror. This resistance was led by Hereward, who succeeded in 1071 in defeating the Normans as they crossed what is now the Old West River. The victory was short lived, and Ely fell to the Normans shortly afterwards.

The name 'Hereward' is used in East Anglia as a rallying call. It has been adopted by Project Hereward, an alliance between the East Anglian Waterways Association and the Peterborough and Great Ouse Branches of the IWA. In the 1970s Project Hereward successfully campaigned to re-open Well Creek to navigation, and is now dedicated to re-opening the Horseway Channel between Horseway Lock and Welches Dam Lock. This will require the relining of the channel to once again hold water.

To restore the link with the Old Bedford River, Welches Dam Lock needs major repair. An innovative alternative idea currently being explored is to preserve the historic Welches Dam Lock in its current form, and build a new lock parallel with it.

In a national perspective, the re-opening of Horseway Channel and Welches Dam Lock is a comparatively simple undertaking compared to other major restoration projects across the Country, however it relies entirely upon the goodwill of the Navigation Authority - the Environment Agency. At the time of writing Project Hereward continues to be reassured by the EA's continuing support.

At its northern end the Old Bedford River passes within a few feet of the Well Creek at Salter's Lode. If a new navigable connection were made here, a 36·5 mile (60km) cruising ring would be created through a re-opened Horseway Channel and Welches Dam Lock, and along the Sixteen Foot and Well Creek, without having to make the difficult entry onto the Old Bedford River through its tidal doors on the Estuary of the River Great Ouse.

Shellfen - the last commercial vessel operating on the Middle Level

The oil tanker *Shellfen* was once a well-known sight on Fenland waterways in winter months. A Westlander Dutch barge built in 1898, and brought over from Holland in 1912 for carrying bulbs grown in Reach Fen to Ely Dock. After this ceased she was used in the general catering trade between Kings Lynn and Cambridge. This too did not last long.

At this time, a start was being made on converting some of the many Fenland pumping stations from steam to diesel operation. Previously gangs of Fenland lighters had supplied the stations with coal and Shell-Mex & BP Ltd bought the barge to carry diesel oil in barrels to the converted pumps. At first she operated on a part-time basis but as the number of engines supplied increased, a full time skipper was appointed. Shortly before the WWII the barge was fitted out as a tanker at Hull and from then on she carried the oil in bulk, pumping it to shore through pipes carried on board.

In 1948 *Shellfen* was based at Appleyard Lincoln's boat yard in Ely, where she operated under contract. Sometime in time in the 1960s ownership was passed to Appleyard Lincoln. At one time over 100 pumping stations were supplied but as the Fen roads were improved, this allowed road tankers to reach them.

Previously inaccessible sites and pumps were converted to all electric working to economise on labour costs, and the number of diesel pumping stations declined. It had fallen to about 80 in 1948 and 50 in 1961. The fuel used to be picked up from Royal tankers at trans-shipment points like Littleport, Chatteris and Benwick Docks, but later road tankers from Kings Lynn arranged to meet the barge at preselected places not far from the pumping stations.

Shellfen is 48 foot long and carried 4,000 gallons. In a wet winter such as 1961 when the pumps were particularly active as many as one 100,000 gallons were supplied. It is generally accepted that Shellfen was the last working boat on the Fens.

In 1970 she was sold to Lorenz & Co. and moved to the Bridgewater Canal. In 1988 she was sold again to a consortium of Morris dancers before being sold to her present owner, the Headley Trust (supported by Sainsbury Family Charitable Trusts). She is on the National Historic Ships Register and was scheduled for restoration restoration in 2019 at the Gloucester shipyard of T Nielsen.

She has her own blog, facebook page, and detailed entry on the National Historic Ships UK Register.

Taken from *Fenland Barge Traffic* by John Wilson and Alan Faulkner

Sixteen Foot Drain: Forty Foot Drain to Popham's Eau

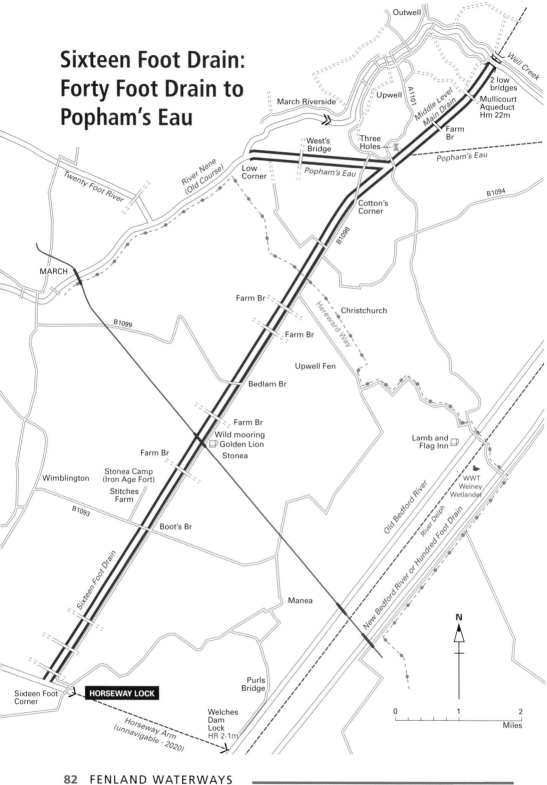

Outwell

Well Creek

2 low bridges

Mullicourt Aqueduct Hm 22m

March Riverside

Upwell

A1101

Middle Level Main Drain

Farm Br

Popham's Eau

West's Bridge

Three Holes

River Nene (Old Course)

Twenty Foot River

Low Corner

Popham's Eau

Cotton's Corner

B1094

B1098

MARCH

Farm Br

Christchurch

B1099

Farm Br

Hereward Way

Upwell Fen

Bedlam Br

Farm Br

Wild mooring

Golden Lion

Stonea

Lamb and Flag Inn

Farm Br

Stonea Camp (Iron Age Fort)

WWT Welney Wetlander

Wimblington

Stitches Farm

Old Bedford River

River Delph

B1093

Boot's Br

New Bedford River or Hundred Foot Drain

Sixteen Foot Drain

Manea

N

Purls Bridge

Sixteen Foot Corner

HORSEWAY LOCK

Welches Dam Lock HR 2·1m

Horseway Arm (unnavigable - 2020)

0   1   2
Miles

Sixteen Foot Drain: Forty Foot Drain to Popham's Eau

Approximate travel time 3·75 hours
Distance 10 miles

Like the Forty Foot or Vermuyden's Drain, the Sixteen Foot Drain is an almost dead straight, wide and deep channel, travelling north-northeast for a total of 12 miles. For a large part it is accompanied by a minor road on its east bank. This isn't as busy as the road alongside the Forty Foot Drain. At the weekend the road is popular with groups of cyclists who usually wave cheerily.

A number of **farm bridges** cross the navigation, **several of which are quite low**. As always, refer to MLC navigation notes for bridge heights, and keep a careful eye on approaching bridges. I set off down the Sixteen Foot Drain one year, with a canoe on top of my narrowboat. I soon realised that a bridge was too low to get under with the canoe on top, and for the rest of the journey I towed it behind me.

After 3 miles you come to **Boot's Bridge** which carries the B1093 between Manea and Wimblington. This bridge was rebuilt and raised during the winter of 2018–19. Access to **Stonea Camp** *(see p. 85)* is a third of a mile west down the B1093.

There are aspirations to provide boating facilities and access to Skylark Garden Centre, café and Sunday car-boot sale, to the west of the Sixteen Foot Drain, below Boot's Bridge.

Another 1·5 miles north the navigation passes under a **railway line**, whilst the nearby road passes under the railway line in a low underpass. Impatient drivers not wanting to wait at the railway level crossing frequently use the underpass without sufficient consideration of the height of their vehicle. The bridge has been dubbed 'Britain's most hit bridge'!

Immediately past the railway bridge is the **Golden Lion PH**. Boaters are always welcome – the pub is almost a 'compulsory stop' on the annual Peterborough IWA Easter cruise! Sadly there are no hard moorings.

We generally send our most nimble crew member up the bank with a mooring pin and spare rope, to create a temporary 'hand rail' to assist others in climbing the bank. As the MLC start to invest the income derived from the charging to use their waters, we hope that providing facilities at locations like this (and The George at Ramsey Forty Foot) will be prioritised.

There are obvious risks in running roads so close to great drains, particularly when those roads are subject to significant subsidence. The Sixteen Foot Drain (like the Forty Foot) has an unfortunate history of vehicles leaving the road and entering the water. A true local hero, Graham Chappell, has been campaigning with considerable success for increased safety on Fenland roads next to water. His campaign is called 'Charlotte's Way' in memory of a young girl who sadly lost her life in 2008.

From the Golden Lion, the navigation continues another 5·25 miles to **Three Holes** and the junction with **Popham's Eau**. The are good moorings at Three Holes (provided by Peterborough Branch IWA). Sadly the village's pub, the Red Hart, had closed down at the time of writing.

Navigators heading for the River Nene (Old Course) will turn left onto Popham's Eau and head west. The eastern branch of Popham's Eau is unnavigable. The Sixteen Foot does

Sixteen Foot Drain

Stonea Camp

Originally a Bronze Age settlement, Stonea became the site of the lowest known Iron Age fort in the country. Now only 6ft above sea level, Stonea would have been an island rising above the flooded fens. It was an important site for the Iceni and may have been the site of a battle in 47 AD reported by Tacitus with a Roman auxiliary force.

After the suppression of Boudicca's rebellion of 60 AD, Stonea was developed as a major camp by the Roman with a large and intimidating stone tower built as a symbol of Roman authority.

Later, as the area settled down, the Romans established administrative centres on the Fosse Way at Godmanchester (Roman name Durovigutum) and Water Newton, near Peterborough (Roman name Durobrivae). The stone tower was demolished and although the larger pieces of stone were removed to other sites for re-use in new buildings, but much of the rubble wasn't cleared, leading to the descriptive, but uncharacteristic for the Fens, name 'Stonea'.

The nearest access is from the Golden Lion on the Sixteen Foot.

continue north for another 2·25 miles to Mullincourt Aqueduct which is effectively the Head of Navigation. The drain continues under the aqueduct and its name changes to the Middle Level Main Drain. Boats are prohibited for this further 8·5 mile stretch to the main pumping station at Wiggenhall St German.

Moorings and facilities

Three Holes moorings provided by Peterborough Branch IWA

Improvise 'wild' moorings at the **Golden Lion PH**

'Wild' mooring outside The Golden Lion on the Sixteen Foot

Stonea Camp Iron Age Hill Fort
Stonea, Wimblington, March PE15 0DU
www.visitcambridgeshirefens.org/stonea-camp-58
For information and talks
☎ 01354 740306

The Golden Lion PH serves food
Sixteen Foot Bank, Stonea, PE15 0DU
☎ 01354 680732

Fen skating

Winter skating on a frozen river or field is a unique experience. The crisp sound underfoot, a sharp wind in your face, cold extremities gradually warming from the glow of exercise. and a sensation akin to flying as the countryside passes by effortlessly. I would compare the differences between the sensation of unrestricted open air skating and the confines of an artificial rink, to the difference between swimming over a coral reef on the Indian ocean and taking a dip in a chlorinated 25m pool!

Skating, using animal bones tied to the bottom of boots, had been employed by Fenland hunters and trappers for centuries. Visiting Dutch drainage engineers in the 17th century brought iron 'schaats' with them which enabled far greater speed and distances to be achieved. On the frozen meres and rivers of the fens skating became enormously popular in the cold winters at the end of the 19th Century (evocatively described by Dickens, and now considered a 'mini ice age')

Thousands of people would attend speed skating matches, and characters with names like William 'Turkey' Smart, his brother 'Fish' Smart, James 'Gutta Perch' See, 'Charger' Legge and 'Swearing Jack' Cooper attracted significant fame (and fortune).

Several Fenland villages claim to be the home to 'bandy' which developed into the modern game of ice hockey.

In 1870 a race was staged between a train travelling the four miles from Littleport to Ely and a skater on the frozen new course of the Great Ouse which ran parallel. It is said that hot coals were thrown from the train onto the ice in an attempt to sabotage the skater, but never-the-less he finished the winner by half a minute!

Old wrought iron fen skates are quite a common site in antique shops. They reveal an interesting sociological perspective. Workers in the 19th century laboured six days a week, with no time for sport or recreation and on the seventh day, the Sabbath, sport was expressly forbidden. However when the factories and mills froze up, unexpected (and unpaid) leisure time was created and skating became possible, using skates strapped onto sturdy working boots.

In the last 20 years there have been very few opportunities for fen skating due to warmer winters and fewer 'freeze ups'. Philippa Pearce's classic children's story *Tom's Midnight Garden* describes a fictional skating trip in Edwardian times along the frozen Rivers Cam and Great Ouse, from what can be identified as Great Shelford, to Ely. The description more powerfully evokes the special experience of Fen Skating than anything else I have ever read!

Popham's Eau: Sixteen Foot Drain to River Nene (Old Course)

Approximate travel time 0·75 hours
Distance 2·3 miles

Originally Popham's Eau was 5·5 miles long, and had a major drainage role. However since the creation of the Middle Level Main Drain the eastern half has become redundant, and is no longer navigable.

From the **Sixteen Foot Drain** at **Three Holes** turn left (west). This perfectly straight navigation, 2 miles long, has little to make it stand out. Nonetheless it plays an important part in moving a lot of water from the west of the Level, and it has a quiet beauty. At the junction with the **River Nene (Old Course)** turn left (southwest) for **March** or right (northeast) to **Marmont Priory Lock** *(see pages 43-48).*

West's Bridge, Popham's Eau

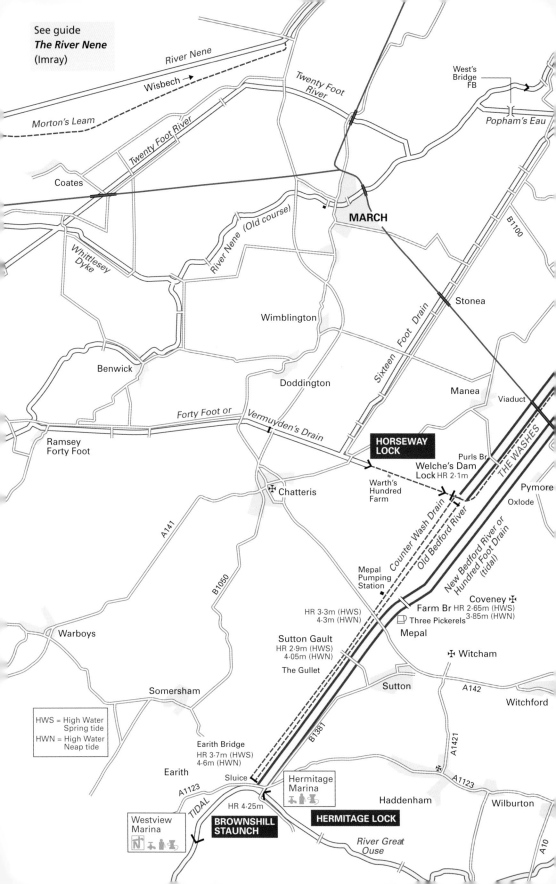

See guide
The River Nene
(Imray)

River Nene

Wisbech →

Morton's Leam

Twenty Foot River

Twenty Foot River

West's Bridge FB

Popham's Eau

Coates

MARCH

B1100

Whittlesey Dyke

River Nene (Old course)

Stonea

Wimblington

Benwick

Sixteen Foot Drain

Doddington

Manea

Viaduct

Forty Foot or Vermuyden's Drain

HORSEWAY LOCK

Purls Br

THE WASHES

Ramsey Forty Foot

Welche's Dam Lock HR 2·1m

Pymore

Oxlode

⚓ Chatteris

Warth's Hundred Farm

Counter Wash Drain

Old Bedford River

New Bedford River or Hundred Foot Drain (tidal)

A141

Mepal Pumping Station

Coveney ✚

Farm Br HR 2·65m (HWS)
3·85m (HWN)

HR 3·3m (HWS)
4·3m (HWN)

☐ Three Pickerels

Warboys

B1050

Sutton Gault
HR 2·9m (HWS)
4·05m (HWN)

Mepal

✚ Witcham

Witchford

A142

The Gullet

Sutton

Somersham

A1421

A1123

HWS = High Water Spring tide
HWN = High Water Neap tide

Earith Bridge
HR 3·7m (HWS)
4·6m (HWN)

B1381

✚

Earith

A1123

Sluice

Hermitage Marina

Haddenham

Wilburton

A10

Westview Marina

TIDAL

HR 4·25m

BROWNSHILL STAUNCH

HERMITAGE LOCK

River Great Ouse

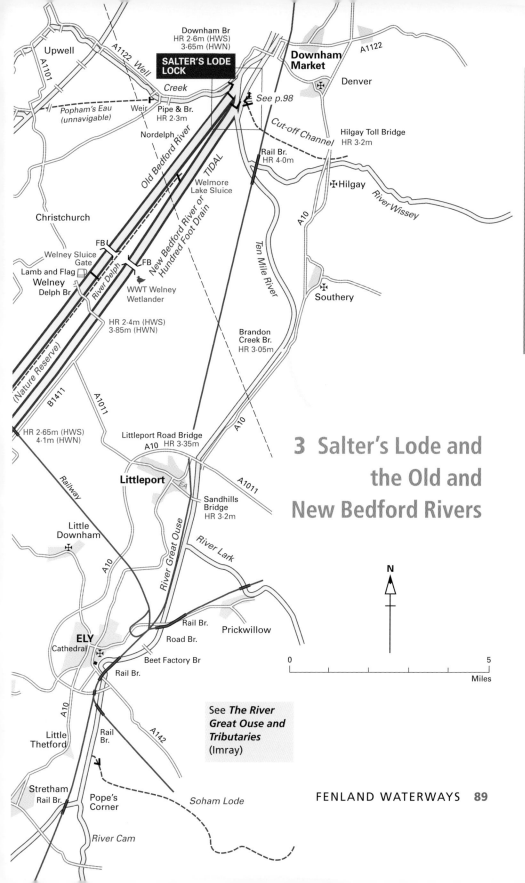

Upwell

Downham Br
HR 2·6m (HWS)
3·65m (HWN)

**SALTER'S LODE
LOCK**

Well   *Creek*

A1122

A1101

Popham's Eau
(unnavigable)   Weir   Pipe & Br.
HR 2·3m

Nordelph

Old Bedford River

Christchurch

FB

Welney Sluice
Gate
Lamb and Flag
Welney
Delph Br

FB

River Delph

TIDAL

Welmore
Lake Sluice

*New Bedford River or
Hundred Foot Drain*

WWT Welney
Wetlander

(Nature Reserve)

HR 2·4m (HWS)
3·85m (HWN)

B1411   A1011

HR 2·65m (HWS)
4·1m (HWN)

Littleport Road Bridge
A10   HR 3·35m

Railway

Littleport

Ten Mile River

A10

Brandon
Creek Br.
HR 3·05m

A1011

EA

Sandhills
Bridge
HR 3·2m

Little
Downham

A10

River Great Ouse

River Lark

**Downham
Market**

A1122

Denver

See p.98

Cut-off Channel

Hilgay Toll Bridge
HR 3·2m

Rail Br.
HR 4·0m

Hilgay

River Wissey

Southery

3 Salter's Lode and
the Old and
New Bedford Rivers

N

0   5
                                Miles

ELY
Cathedral

Rail Br.   Road Br.

Beet Factory Br

Rail Br.

A10

Little
Thetford

Rail
Br.

A142

Stretham
Rail Br.

Pope's
Corner

River Cam

Prickwillow

See *The River
Great Ouse and
Tributaries*
(Imray)

Soham Lode

FENLAND WATERWAYS   **89**

Welches Dam

SALTER'S LODE AND THE OLD AND NEW BEDFORD RIVERS

Old Bedford River: Salter's Lode to Welches Dam

Approximate travel time 2·5–3 hours
Distance 12 miles

The navigation authority for both the Old Bedford River and New Bedford River (aka Hundred Foot Drain) is the Environment Agency. To navigate either you need an appropriate registration (either an EA registration, or a combined EA + CRT Gold Licence).

Prior to the re-opening in the 1970s of Well Creek, the through route between the rivers Nene and Great Ouse involved navigating the Old Bedford River. This was accessed by continuing east where the Forty Foot meets the Sixteen Foot, passing through Horseway Lock and the two miles along Horseway Channel to Welches Dam Lock.

Undredged creek giving access to the Old Bedford River

Immediately after the lock, one turned left (north) onto the Old Bedford River (this being the Head of Navigation, the southern part of the river being unnavigable).

The Horseway Channel had a long history of leaking and access was only periodical, when it was temporarily refilled. In 2006 the EA piled across the face of Welches Dam Lock to prevent water leaking from the Old Bedford River under the lock cill into the already leaking Horseway Channel. This action closed navigation.

The Old Bedford River outflows into the estuary of the Great Ouse through a double sluice just south of Salter's Lode Lock, and since the closure of Welches Dam Lock this is the only access to the Old Bedford River.

Access is through first a pair of sea doors, and almost immediately behind them, a guillotine gate.

The Old Bedford River serves both as a drainage channel in winter, and an irrigation source in summer. A key consideration in opening the sea doors and guillotine gate is to ensure that salt water from the estuary doesn't get into

Leaving the Old Bedford River

countryside. The river is almost completely straight.

After 3 miles you pass under a great line of pylons (the same line that you pass under on both Well Creek (west of Nordelph) and the Great Ouse (above Littleport). A further 2·75 miles you pass under **Welney Sluice** (check in advance with EA that the sluice will be open). You can moor here and visit the **Lamb and Flag PH** in **Welney**, which is situated beside the A1011 that crosses the River and runs through the centre of Welney. The Lamb and Flag is another pub known for its warm welcome to boaters!

the Old Bedford River. Although the crops irrigated by water pumped from the Old Bedford River are often potatoes, which may well be sold for crisps, the growers don't want them 'ready salted' at quite so early a stage!

Entry onto the Old Bedford can be made on neap tides by prior arrangement, and with the support of the EA. Due to siltation below the sluices, this can sometimes involve entering the channel backwards, beaching, and cutting a route through the mud with your propellor! Under the tutelage of the intrepid 'go-everywhere' boater, John Revell, I have done this several times.

Although getting onto the Old Bedford is difficult in the extreme, travelling the 12 miles to Welches Dam Lock can be both interesting and rewarding, so long as the water levels are reasonably high and the cot weed not too extreme.

Unlike other Fenland rivers the western bank of the river is not built up above eye level, and there are fine views of the

Welney Sluice

Old Bedford River, 'Meccano' railway bridge

From **Welney road bridge** to the 'Meccano' railway bridge is a further 3·5 miles. To your right, approximately half way along the stretch, is the now abandoned **Manea Colony** *(see p. 96)*.

Welches Dam Lock is another 2·5 miles beyond the 'Meccano' bridge.

At **Welches Dam** there are three houses, two of which are former pubs. Although there is no winding hole, we've turned a 60ft narrowboat without difficulty. The return trip to the V gates and sluice at Salter's Lode is a total of 12 miles.

I've made this trip three times, and despite the difficulty of getting on and off the Old Bedford River, thoroughly enjoyed it.

There is a campaign *(see* Project Hereward, *p. 80)* to reopen Horseway Channel and Welches Dam Lock, which would once again allow non-estuary access to the Old Bedford River. At Salter's Lode the Old Bedford River is only a couple of boat lengths distant from the Well Creek. If a connection were made at Salter's Lode a 36 mile cruising ring would be created without any of the excitement of getting in and out of the estuary.)

Proving the curvature of the earth on the Old Bedford River

From the secure perspective of the 21st century we all know which camp we belong to, Zetetics or Globularists. No longer do heated arguments rage in the pub over whether the Earth is flat (Zetetic) or round (Globularist). However in the 19th century this important concern was a hot subject for debate. Thanks to its straightness the Old Bedford River became the proving ground for the counter arguments.

In 1838 Samuel Rowbotham endeavoured to prove the earth flat by making observations along the 6 mile straight above Welney. Using a telescope he observed barges six miles away. Samuel argued that if the earth was round (as some scientists then argued) the barges would only be visible for 3 miles before they disappeared from sight due to the curvature of the Earth. As he could still make out the barges 6 miles distant, *ipso facto* there was no curve.

This 'proof' stood unchallenged until 1870 when Alfred Russel Wallace, inspired to renewed scientific scrutiny by Charles Darwin's work on evolution, conducted a further experiment on the Old Bedford River. Three barges, each with a pole of identical length erected on them, were moored at 2 mile intervals. If the earth was flat, the tops of the three rods would line up when observed through a telescope. However the second marker was a clear 32 inches above a line between the first and third markers, proving, *quod erat demonstrandum,* the curvature of the Earth.

We now understand that Rowbotham's apparent ability to see further than the expected 3 miles was caused by the phenomenon of the refraction (bending) of light over water.

Remarkably, the measurements employed in the 19th century to calculate the diameter of the earth arrived at a figure of 7,920 miles. With the benefits of modern scientific instrumentation, the diameter of the earth at the equator is now stated to be 7,926 miles!

Manea Colony

Social discontent and change often follow after periods of major warfare. In the UK the 1945 election of Clement Atlee's Labour Government at the end of WWII was a prime example. Another great European struggle, the Napoleonic Wars (1803–1815), led to a considerable period of turbulence in Britain.

The economy had suffered from years of war, thousands of ex-soldiers flooded the labour market, causing wages to fall below subsidence levels. Rioting became common place, including the infamous 1816 Littleport riots. The expanding Industrial Revolution and introduction of machinery threatened workers, the 1834 amendment to the Poor Laws broke up families by segregating workhouses.

Against this troubled background socialism flourished, demanding universal suffrage for men. Robert Owen painted a vision of a 'communitarian' society promoting an Utopian socialist economic vision of a new moral world, and across the Country 'Chartist' communities were set up.

In 1838 a local farmer and Methodist Minister, William Hodson, resolved to create a socialist colony by building a small township on the west bank of the Old Bedford River on 200 acres of land at Manea Fen, now known as the

A view of the colony published in the 'Working Bee', the community's weekly newspaper

Manea Fifties. The community started, making its own bricks to build a Church, houses, workshops, a community building, a school, a large pavilion and a windmill. They produced a newspaper, the 'Working Bee'.

Sadly the dream didn't last. Disputes broke out within the community, and in 1841 William Hodson withdrew his financial support, and within a couple of years the colonists had all gone. People carried on living in the houses, digging clay and making bricks but occupation gradually dwindled. The 1851 census recorded 74 people living there, the 1881 census 27, and the last record to be found is of a baptism in 1906. The abandoned brick pits flooded and were shown as swamps on the 1890 Ordnance Survey map.

Mepal Washes

Fenland's Floating Church

In the 19th century the only way agricultural workers in remote Fenland villages went anywhere was by walking. In 1896 the Vicar of Stretham resolved that if people couldn't easily get to church, he would take the church to the people.

He acquired three horse drawn wagons and sent them out into the Archdeaconary of Huntingdon as travelling churches. This experiment was largely successful, except in the Fens where often the roads and droves were impassable in summer due to deep ruts, and in winter because of mud. Although travelling churches provided a solution for much of Huntingdonshire, it was clear that something else was necessary to take religion into the less accessible parts of the Fens.

In 1896 a floating church was commissioned to serve the Fenland parish of Holme. At the time Holme had 42 houses spread over a distance of between two and four miles from the parish church by road, whereas they were all within one mile of the river, and 26 of them practically bankside.

Built at Stanground, outside Peterborough, the Floating Church was launched in April 1897. She was dedicated to St Withburga, daughter of Anna, King of the Angles, and likely sister to both St Etheldreda of Ely and St Wendreda of March.

Unable to ring bells from a conventional spire (which wouldn't have fitted under the low fenland bridges), the Floating Church (or 'Ark' as it came to be known) flew two flags, those of St Andrew & St George, to announce that services were about to start. Between its launch and October 1904, a choir was formed, needlework and bible classes held, and 74 baptisms are recorded as having taken place on board.

The Floating Church at her moorings in Stokes' Yard 1897 *The Fenland Ark*, John Bennett

In 1905 the barge was sold to the parish of Manea to serve Welches Dam, Purl's Bridge and the former Colony at Manea, all isolated communities next to the Old Bedford River. However the houses at the Colony were abandoned with a year and the congregation shrank to an unsustainable level.

In 1907 the barge was abandoned near Ramsey St Mary before being sold off to a group of young men who renamed it 'Saint's Rest', converted it into a houseboat, and moored it near Orton Staunch where Peterborough Yacht Club's moorings now are. During severe flooding, probably in August 1912, she finally sank.

The Floating Church, with flags showing a service is about to start, at Allen's Engine 1903

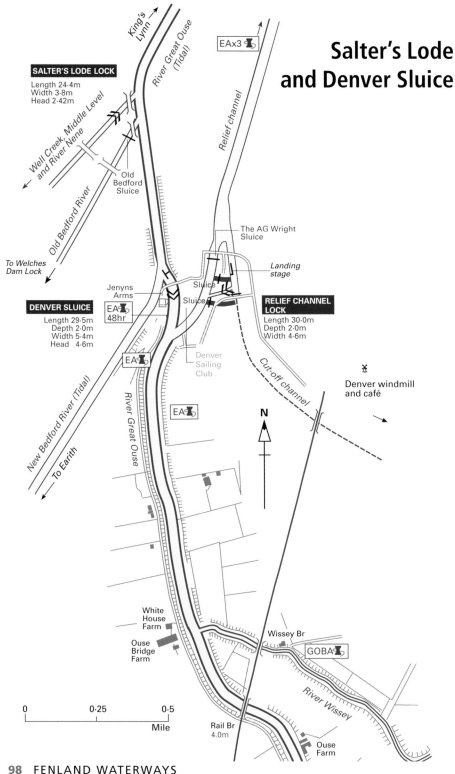

Salter's Lode and Denver Sluice

SALTER'S LODE LOCK
Length 24·4m
Width 3·8m
Head 2·42m

EAx3

King's Lynn

River Great Ouse (Tidal)

Relief channel

Well Creek, Middle Level and River Nene

Old Bedford Sluice

Old Bedford River

To Welches Dam Lock

The AG Wright Sluice

Landing stage

Jenyns Arms

Sluice

Sluice

EA 48hr

DENVER SLUICE
Length 29·5m
Depth 2·0m
Width 5·4m
Head 4·6m

RELIEF CHANNEL LOCK
Length 30·0m
Depth 2·0m
Width 4·6m

EA

Denver Sailing Club

EA

New Bedford River (Tidal)

To Earith

River Great Ouse

Cut-off channel

Denver windmill and café

N

White House Farm

Ouse Bridge Farm

Wissey Br

GOBA

River Wissey

0   0·25   0·5
Mile

Rail Br 4.0m

Ouse Farm

New Bedford River: Denver to Earith

Approximate travel time 4·25 hours
Distance 20 miles

The **New Bedford River** is a man-made tidal cut, forming a direct link between **Earith** and the estuary of the **Great Ouse** immediately below **Denver Sluice**. Although it offers something of a 'short cut' between Denver and Earith, advice should be taken from the lock keepers at either Salter's Lode, or Denver before boating it. The journey is best done on specific tides as advised by the lock keeper. It is recommended to make the journey upstream, from Denver to Earith, on a rising tide. If you try boating downstream on a falling tide, waiting for the tide to fall sufficiently to get under the A1123 road bridge at

Denver

Beaten by the outgoing tide - stuck on the New Bedford River

Earith will probably mean 'running out of water' before reaching the A1101 road bridge at Welney. It is quite common for boats to get temporarily stuck thereabouts, either as a result of the tide going out too quickly and 'beaching' a boat, or the tide coming in too quickly through 'the Narrows' and just bringing the boat to a halt. In either case waiting patiently for tidal conditions to change is the only option. Any time saving from this apparent short cut is easily lost.

The popular **Three Pickerels PH** is in **Mepal**, but moorings need to be improvised, and water levels can alter significantly during the time it takes to enjoy a meal.

I wouldn't say 'don't navigate the New Bedford River', but it's not for the faint hearted! The alternative, longer but more comfortable, route takes you through the beautiful cathedral city of Ely, and offers significantly more revictualling opportunities.

This journey is susceptible to the changing nature of tides and weather.

The times and conditions described below record one particular journey the author made in September 2019 in the company of Mike Daines and John Revell on John's boat *Olive Emily*, a 43 foot 43hp steel narrowboat, and are not typical of all journeys.

John Revell and *Olive Emily*

We left **Salter's Lode Lock** at the bottom of a spring tide, as soon as there was sufficient depth of water. (Had we left from Denver Lock we would have been delayed by having to wait for the water to clear the sand bar below the sluices.)

When we entered the New Bedford River the tide was coming in quite fast and we were travelling at 7mph on low (1200rpm) engine revs. There was a lot of floating debris in the water around us, but it was

Welmore Lake sluice

flowing on the tide in the same direction as us, so it didn't cause a problem.

We passed **Welmore Lake sluice** after 1·6 miles, taking care to avoid the sandbank below the sluice. One and half miles later we passed under the pylons and and in a further mile and a half passed **Welney Wetland Centre** and under their pedestrian bridge (which is covered to conceal visiting humans from birds).

By the time we reached the **A1101 road bridge**, another 1·3miles, we had been travelling just over 2 hours. Just under another hour later we passed under the **'Meccano' railway bridge** a further 3·35 miles on. The water was by now largely debris free, and the tide had stopped coming in.

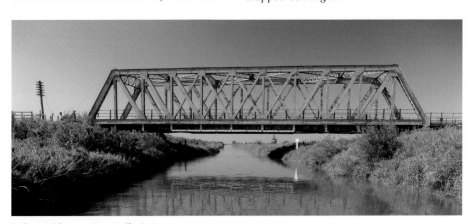

Railway Bridge over New Bedford River

Six miles on we passed under the **old bridge at Mepal** by the 'Three Pickerels'. Sadly there are no proper moorings to facilitate accessing the pub, but determined boaters have been known to improvise!

Shortly afterwards came the modern concrete causeway carrying Ireton's Way (A142). The eponymous Ireton's Way was built on the instruction of Cromwell's General Ireton. Immediately west of the bridge are the remains of a grass sided lock which once linked the Old and New Bedford Rivers.

Two miles on we passed by the The Anchor PH at Sutton Gault, again, unfortunately no moorings and the pub is now closed and seems unlikely to reopen.

If by now the tide was beginning to turn it was barely noticeable, the river being wide and full.

3·8 miles later we passed under the **A1123 bridge at Earith** and came to rest on **Hermitage Lock moorings.**

The entire 20 mile journey down the Old Bedford River (or Hundred Foot Drain) had taken 4·25 hours. In comparison the alternative route along the Great Ouse and Old West River is a total distance of 30 miles, and on average takes 8 hours.

See guide
The River Great Ouse and Tributaries
(Imray)

Mepal bridge

The Ouse Washes

The Ouse Washes are a 10 square mile nature reserve of international importance. They are protected by an comprehensive series of classifications. They are a SSSI (site of special scientific interest), a Ramsar important wetland site (Ramsar is a 1975 intergovernmental environmental treaty), a SPA (special protection area) under the European Union Birds Directive, a Special Area of Conservation and a Grade 1 Nature Conservation Review Site.

The Washes form a flood-plain lying between the Old Bedford River/Delph River and the New Bedford River, stretching from St Ives in the south west to Downham Market in the north east. With the capacity to store a staggering 20,000 million gallons of water, they are fed from the river Great Ouse via the Old Bedford River (which becomes the River Delph) before the waters spill out onto the flood plain. When the waters are released at the northern end, they are let out into the New Bedford River through Welmore Lake Sluice back into the tidal Great Ouse where they finally flow out to sea.

The RSPB have observational hides at Purl's Bridge (accessed from Manea down what must surely be the bumpiest road in Cambridgeshire). Facilities are basic, but there are toilets.

Ouse Washes

Welney Wetland Centre (wwt.org.uk) is an altogether grander (and warmer) affair, with a restaurant and shop, and an enclosed bridge crossing the New Bedford River to the observation areas.

In winter the washes attract thousands of ducks & swans, and in spring they are a breeding ground for hundreds of snipe, lapwings and redshanks. Even a non-twitcher, like me, has been pleasantly surprised by what an fascinating and enthralling day can be had there.

As well as providing a varied and rich ecosystem, the Washes are a fantastic leisure resource. I've walked the banks of the New Bedford River in Summer, paddled across the flooded washes in Autumn, and hope one day to skate them.

As autumn turns into winter it is worth stopping at Salter's Lode and walking along the bank of the New Bedford River. You will be treated to the spectacle of flocks of birds arriving from Arctic Russia and Iceland. They land with an apparent sense of relief and exhaustion that can only result from flying several thousand miles in near freezing conditions.

Sutton Washes

Fenland hover train experiment

In 1966 the introduction of two cross-channel hovercraft services raised public awareness in hovercraft. By 1968 car carrying cross-channel craft led to 'hovering' becoming 'all the rage' and in 1969 the Government initiated experiments in an innovative 'Tracked Hovercraft'. To facilitate this a 1 mile long experimental track was built along the side of the Old Bedford River between Sutton Gault and Earith.

The intent was for a train, hovering 6 inches above the track, to run at speeds up to 300mph, and a golden era of super fast rail travel was envisaged, with travel times between Glasgow and London dropping from around 6 hours to little more than two hours.

In 1966 a British Pathé news film boasted: 'Like to travel by train at 300mph? We may do in a few years time! Forget about wheels, the hovercraft principle, with a train supported by an air cushion and skimming over a magnetic field at near aircraft speed, is a dream no longer.'

On 7 February 1973 a speed of 104mph (into a 20mph head wind) was achieved, but the experiment was already running into trouble. Alternative Maglev (magnetic levitation) technology was being developed and the Japanese were developing their own bullet

One of the concrete support pillars on the Old Bedford Counter Wash Drain

train (which would eventually achieve speeds of 275mph in the 1990s)

Advances were being made with the UK's other experiment in high speed rail travel, the APT (Advanced Passenger Train) and the Minister for Aerospace and Shipping, Michael Heseltine 'pulled the plug' on the Tracked Hovercraft.

Little evidence remains today to testify to this bold technological attempt to lead the world. There are three concrete support pillars that still stand forlornly sticking out of the ground just north of Earith, whilst the engine RTV31 (research test vehicle 31) is preserved at Peterborough Railworld Wildlife Haven close to the banks of the River Nene and just yards away from the main railway line.

Hover train research test vehicle at Peterborough

APPENDIX

References and further reading

The Fens, Francis Pryor, 2019 (Head of Zeus)

The story of the Fens, Frank Meeres, 2019 (The History Press)

Outwell in a nutshell, William P Smith, 2017 (Carrillson Publications)

Exploring the Fen Edge: along the Roman Car Dyke, Rex Sly, 2017 (Jellyfish Solutions)

The Anglo Saxon Fenland, Susan Oosthuizen, 2017 (Windgatherer Press)

Charlie Fox, building a legacy, Emily Syred, 2014 (Fox Narrowboats)

A pictorial journey down the Wisbech Canal, William P Smith, 2014 (Carrillson Publications)

The Lost Fens, Ian Rotherham, 2013 (The History Press)

The Cambridgeshire Fens, Trevor Bevis and Malcolm Allen, 2010

Inland Waterways of Great Britain, Jane Cumberlidge, 2009 (Imray)

Well Creek - The Story of a Waterway, William P Smith, 2008 (Well Creek Trust)

Lost Tramways of East Anglia, Leslie Oppitz, 2004 (Countryside Books)

Prisoners of the Fens, Trevor Bevis, 2003, published by the author

From punt to plough, Rex Sly, 2003 (The History Press)

A Level Country, Andrew Hunter Blair, 2003, (John Nickalls)

The Story of the Fens, Valerie Gerrard, 2003 (Robert Hale)

England's Thousand Best Churches, Simon Jenkins, 1999 (Penguin Group)

Times of Flood, Anthony Day, 1997 (S B Publications)

The Memorial Church of St Wendreda, March, Trevor Bevis, 1996 (Published by the Author)

A Fenland Christmas, Chris Carling, 1990

Taming the flood, Jeremy Purseglove, 1988 (Oxford University Press)

Lord Orford's voyage around the Fens in 1774, intr. H J K Jenkins, 1987

Memoirs of a Fen Tiger, Audrey James, 1986 (David and Charles)

Memoirs of a Fenland mole catcher, Bill 'Pop' Bowles, 1986 (Cambridgeshire Libraries)

Spirit of the Fens, Edward Storey, 1985 (Robert Hale)

Waterland, Graham Swift (fiction) 1983, (William Heinmann)

The Changing Fenland, H C Darby, 1983 (Cambridge University Press)

Fenland: its ancient past and uncertain future, Harry Godwin, 1978

Call it a Summer County, Edward Storey, 1978 (Robert Hale)

The Canals of Eastern England, John Boyes and Ronald Russel, 1977 (David & Charles)

The Great Level, Dorothy Summers, 1976 (David & Charles)

The Fenland, A K Parker & D Pyle, 1976 (David & Charles)

Fenwomen, Mary Chamberlain, 1975 (Virago)

The Solitary Landscape, Edward Storey, 1975 (Victor Gollancz)

Fenland Rivers, Alan & Michael Roulstone, 1974 (Balfour)

Rum Owd Boys, James Wentworth Day, 1974 (East Anglian Magazine Pubs.)

Portrait of the Fen County, Edward Storey, 1971 (Robert Hale)

History of The Fens, James Wentworth Day, 1970 (George Harrap & Co)

Fenland Memories, Arthur Randell, 1969 (Routledge & Kegan Paul)

Fenland Chronicle, Sybil Marshall, 1967

Sixty Years a Feynman, Arthur Randall, 1966 (Routledge & Kegan Paul)

More Tales from The Fens, W H Barrett, 1964 (Routledge & Kegan Paul)

Tales from The Fens, W H Barrett, 1963 (Routledge & Kegan Paul)

A Fenman's story, W H Barrett, 1965 (Routledge & Kegan Paul)

Tom's Midnight Garden, Philippa Pearce, 1958

The skaters of the Fens, Alan Bloom, 1957 (W Heffer & Sons, Cambridge)

The Black Fens, A K Astbury, 1957 (County History Reprints - 1970)

The Buildings of England, Cambridgeshire, N Pevsner, 1954

The Fens, Alan Bloom, 1953 (Robert Hale)

Cambridgeshire: Huntingdonshire and the Isle of Ely, E A R Ennion, 1951

The Medieval Fenland, H C Darby, 1940 (David & Charles)

The Draining of the Fens, H C Darby, 1940 (Cambridge University Press)

Bradshaw's Canals and Navigable Rivers, Henry de Salis,1904, (David and Charles reprint –1969)

The Fenland, Past and Present, S H Miller & S Skertchly, 1878

Dorothy L Sayers

Dorothy L Sayers (1893–1957), one of the 'Queens of Crime' in The Golden Age of Detective Fiction, grew up in first in Bluntisham, and later in Christchurch where her father was Rector. The family seat of her aristocratic fictional detective, Lord Peter Wimsey, was Denver.

Wimsey helped defend his brother, the 16th Duke of Denver, when he became the chief murder suspect in Sayers' novel Clouds of Witnesses in which he was tried by his peers, before the full House of Lords. Her choice of the name 'Denver' for the fictional Dukedom reflects her Fenland roots.

Her 1934 mystery the award winning The Nine Tailors is set in the fictional fenland village of Fenchurch St Paul. The end of the book includes a vivid description of a massive flood, and it is hard to avoid the conclusion that Sayers must herself have witnessed similar flooding while growing up in the Fens.

It has been suggested that several characters in the book share names with gravestones in Bluntisham churchyard.

Page numbers in **bold** refer to maps

Index

Index